BARCLAYS PREMIER LEAGUE
CHAMPIONS
2014-15

Photography: Darren Walsh, AP Images, PA Pics
Production: Roy Gilfoyle
Writers: Richard Godden, James Cleary
Design: Glen Hind, Alison Barkley, Lee Ashun, Colin Sumpter
Cover design: Colin Harrison
Statistics: Paul Dutton
Thanks to: David Antill, Andy Jones, Kevin Newman

Produced by Trinity Mirror Sport Media
Managing Director: Steve Hanrahan
Executive Art Editor: Rick Cooke
Executive Editor: Paul Dove

Published in Great Britain in 2015 by: Trinity Mirror Sport Media,
PO Box 48, Old Hall Street, Liverpool L69 3EB.
Copyright of Chelsea Football Club.

ISBN: 9781910335239

Printed by KINT Ljubljana

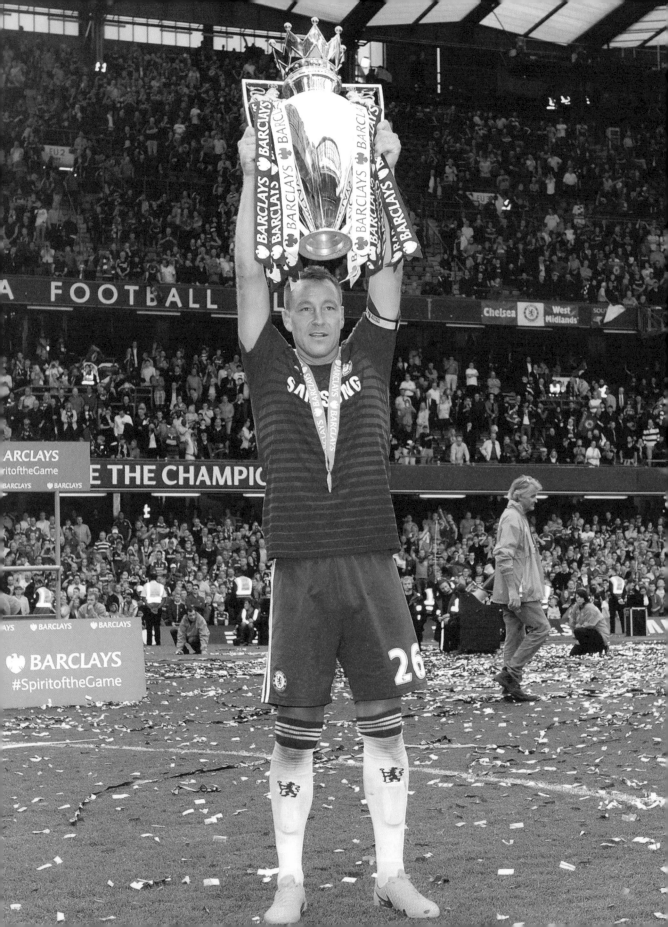

CONTENTS

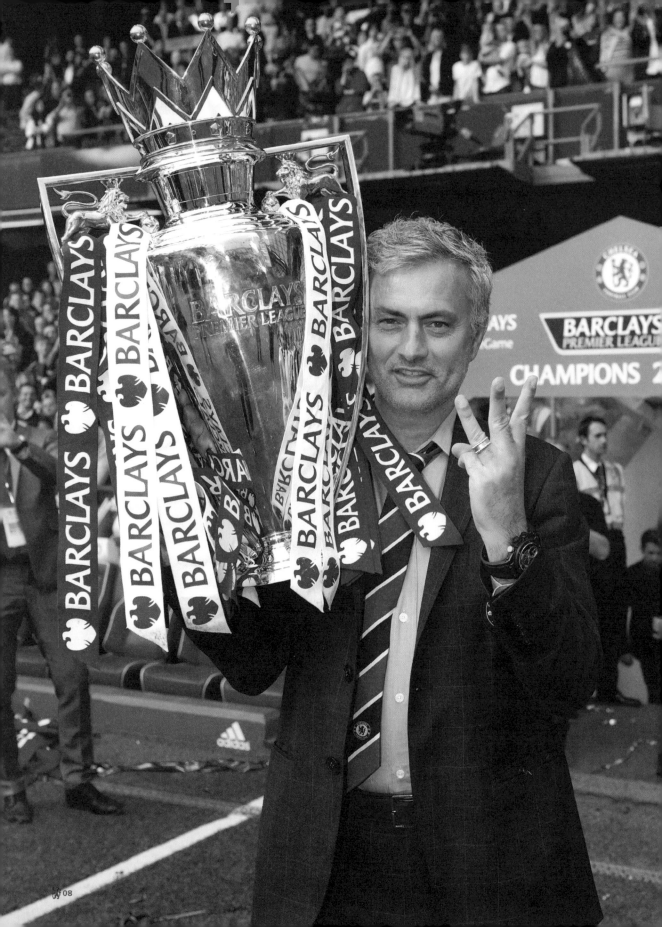

JOSE MOURINHO

'This is a special feeling'

Every one of us in the Chelsea family is a champion.

Chelsea FC are champions again. I am happy, I am proud and I don't forget my people.

My people are my family, but my people are also my Chelsea family: my players; my assistants; my medical department; my kit men; my analysis department, and everyone at the club working day by day to give us the best conditions – my boss, my board, the people who decided to bring me back.

You supporters, I think you also had some responsibility for my return, so I want to share my happiness and my pride with you all and I want to thank you. It is our title – time to enjoy it, time to celebrate it.

When you work so hard and you are champions you feel you got what you deserved, it's a good feeling. For me, it may be a special feeling because I'm not the smartest guy when it comes to choosing countries and clubs. I chose the most difficult league in Europe, I chose a club where I was happy before. I'm so happy to win another Premier League title in my second spell at the club. I will try for another one. The day I don't feel the pressure to do it again, I will stop. What the players are feeling is fantastic, they deserve it and now they can relax.

We were convinced for a long time that we could do it but my experience and maturity was always present and in control of the situation.

We are champions now but during the season we had some crucial moments we coped with in a fantastic way. On 1 January when we were level on points with Manchester City after a heavy defeat at Spurs. Instead of being a turning point it was our last defeat until we were confirmed as champions. Everybody knows we deserve it.

We showed absolutely everything football demands from a team since day one; fantastic attacking football, fantastic domination, high percentages of ball possession, low percentages of ball possession, we gave the ball to the opponents strategically, we defended well. We did everything a team needs to do. That's why we are champions.

JOSE MOURINHO

In England everybody wants the same but only one can win. It doesn't mean the others are not doing good work. It's difficult.

You go to other countries and you know that if you have a top team you win. In this country you can finish first, fourth or fifth.

We were third, now we are first. It's dangerous but we must always think positively and start the season feeling we are title contenders, but after that there is a big risk.

The Premier League is a completely different competition to other leagues I've worked in. I'm not saying Real Madrid and Barcelona couldn't be champions here; obviously they could. But it's not just the difference in quality, there is a difference in mentality. In Spain the smaller teams don't think they

can beat the big ones so they don't compete.

We have improved. We have gone from third to first – two very important steps, and probably the most difficult steps. The most difficult step is the one that makes you champions, and we have made that step.

I want to develop this team. Last year I was keen to see some people leave and for the club to raise funds. This season I'm so happy with what my team gave me that what's fundamental is to keep my players and try to get the best out of them.

I'm happy with my squad and I have to respect the people that gave us the title.

Comparing my Chelsea titles, the first one was difficult because it was our first one in the Premier League. The second one our team was so strong and

JOSE MOURINHO

stable, with so many big players in the best years of their careers. This one is completely different, the league is different, Chelsea are different, opponents are different. My team is one where so many of them have won the league for the first time; that's something they have to learn to do.

I won titles in Spain and Portugal but the ones at Chelsea were fantastic because it was the beginning of Mr Abramovich's era with no title before that. Now, for me, it is a great feeling because it is my club, because of the league and because we are not any more the rich club. We are a top club but a club that lives from the work everyone does in this club.

When you have the taste of success, the big players

want more. There are people who are happy with just one victory but the big ones don't get tired of winning. So I hope really that these players get a good taste which is maybe why the Capital One Cup was important for the group. We won a trophy and enjoyed Wembley, enjoyed the happiness of the supporters.

The teams of 2004/05 and 2005/06, and also after that, were fantastic teams and players. This team is at the beginning, they have won one Capital One Cup and one Premier League. They have to win more to be better than that.

You can win something in a certain moment and that's it, or you can win on a regular basis, that's what makes the difference. Let's try to motivate them to do that.

OUR BOSS IS A WINNER

John Terry:

"He has been different class all year; he deserves a lot of respect. He is the best by a long way. We were the best side footballing-wise up to Christmas and then teams made it difficult, and he found a way to win.

"If you don't show hunger and desire every day you won't play, he [Mourinho] makes that very clear from day one. To keep winning trophies year after year, and keep that hunger inside the belly, is an example to everyone."

Cesc Fàbregas:

"He loves winning. He has some edge that goes above anyone I have been with, a mentality he shows in every single training session and in every game. I can now understand why he has won what he has won in his career."

Thibaut Courtois:

"Working for him now, it is easy to see why his sides have that fighting mentality. He motivates you. He knows when to be among his players, as 'one of us' making jokes, and when to be strong and distant, even severe. That's how it has to be to get the team sharp."

Branislav Ivanovic:

"He is, for sure, the best manager. In every game he has crucial things to say and he always makes the difference."

MOURINHO'S MEN

John Terry

Our record-breaking skipper had another superb year at the club he loves so much.

Not only did he lift the Premier League and Capital One Cup trophies, he looked as good as ever, chipped in with several important goals, and he also captained his beloved Chelsea for the 500th time in October.

Terry's career was revitalised by the return of José Mourinho in the summer of 2013.

Our Portuguese manager has immense faith in his captain and made him a mainstay in the team, once again resulting in a solid campaign from Terry in 2013/14, but he reached even greater heights last term.

His organisation and all-round defensive abilities have never been in doubt and he has always contributed more than his fair share of goals. Indeed,

he equalled his best goals tally in a season, registering eight in 2014/15.

Last year he chipped in with important strikes in the 2-0 wins at Stoke and at home to West Ham and he even came up with a Wembley goal as he opened the scoring against Tottenham in the Capital One Cup final – his first cup final goal for the club.

His goals helped him to become the highest-scoring defender in Premier League history as his strike against Liverpool in May made it 39 in English football's top division.

It's hard to imagine life at Chelsea without a man who has such an affinity with the club and a close bond with the fans, and his loyalty and class has been rewarded with a contract extension.

So there's a chance we'll be able to see JT lifting more silverware as Chelsea skipper in the future.

"I AM STILL CAPTAIN AND I AM STILL HUNGRY TO WIN THINGS AND HOPEFULLY THAT PASSION NEVER GOES"

MOURINHO'S MEN TERRY

661 APPEARANCES, 63 GOALS

JOSE SAYS...

"He's always been able to score goals, normally four or five goals a season. He's full of confidence. I see my John of 2004, 2005 and 2006 here; I don't see any difference. He's playing so well but when the team is playing so well it's easy for individuals."

STATS...

John Terry was a mainstay of the Chelsea team once again in his 17th season with the first-team. He has now skippered the team well over 500 times and has chipped in with his customary contribution of goals, clocking up eight in all competitions last campaign. He played every minute of every game of the Barclays Premier League season and managed 49 appearances overall.

JOHN TERRY

Position: Defender

Date of birth: 07.12.80

Place of birth: Barking

2014/15 PREMIER LEAGUE	
Appearances	38
Minutes	3654
Goals	5
Assists	1

Assists are judged not for the last touch but by the subjective view of the club statistician for a crucial part played in the goal. Minutes include stoppage time.

MOURINHO'S MEN

Oscar

Being entrusted with the No8 shirt brings great responsibility around Stamford Bridge.

That's the number worn previously by club legend Frank Lampard but Oscar took the shirt, stepped up and had an influential season.

A regular in the side, Oscar impressed, often operating in a central role behind the lone frontman, contributing a number of goals.

The match-winner in the victory over Bolton Wanderers that put the Blues on the road to Capital One Cup glory, three days later he got his first in the league in a 3-0 victory over Aston Villa.

His 25-yard free-kick at Crystal Palace was special, swerving beyond the dive of Eagles goalkeeper Julian Speroni, and then there was a fine first-time angled drive with the outside of his right foot, the opener in the 2-1 west London derby victory over QPR, which clinched the Chelsea goal of the season.

He made his 100th start for the club on New Year's Day at Spurs before opening the scoring in the 2-0 defeat of Newcastle United to set the Blues on our way to a 10th successive home league win. Seven days later he scored after only 50 seconds – the first of two goals – as Chelsea cruised to a 5-0 victory at Swansea City.

Oscar also added a Capital One Cup winners' medal to his growing collection, coming off the bench as Tottenham were defeated 2-0.

His final contribution was a painful one, suffering concussion following his collision with Arsenal goalkeeper David Ospina in the crucial 0-0 draw at the Gunners in late April.

MOURINHO'S MEN OSCAR

"THIS SQUAD IS REALLY YOUNG AND WE'VE BEEN PLAYING TOGETHER FOR A LONG TIME. WE ARE IMPROVING AS TIME GOES BY"

JOSE SAYS...

"He's not a number 10 that plays with the ball at his feet, he's a number 10 that looks back, looks to the side, analyses the game and sees where the team needs him to move to get the ball and also to create balance."

MOURINHO'S MEN OSCAR

STATS...

Oscar made 26 Premier League starts plus two as a substitute, scoring six goals. He also made seven appearances in the Champions League, two in the FA Cup and four in the Capital One Cup (one goal).

OSCAR
Position: Midfielder
Date of birth: 09.09.91
Place of birth: Americana, Brazil

2014/15 PREMIER LEAGUE	
Appearances	26+2
Minutes	2112
Goals	6
Assists	10

Nemanja Matic

Having previously been with the Blues from August 2009 to January 2011, Matic rejoined Chelsea in January 2014. Since then, the Serbian has played a pivotal role at the centre of José Mourinho's trophy-chasing side.

The rangy midfielder enjoyed an outstanding start to the 2014/15 campaign and was a virtual ever-present in the league side that topped the table throughout the campaign.

Indeed, his consistency was mirrored by the team as his assured performances as a defence-minded linchpin allowed the more creative influences the freedom to express themselves.

He scored his first goal for the club in a 6-3 win at Everton in August and followed that up with European strikes against Sporting Lisbon and Maribor away.

Building a solid partnership in central midfield alongside Cesc Fàbregas, Matic impressed to such an extent that he was named in the 2014/15 PFA Team of the Season, one of six Chelsea players to be selected.

It may be a coincidence but Matic was an ever-present in the team until December when he missed the Newcastle game through suspension – the first match Chelsea lost all season.

He made his 50th appearance in a Chelsea shirt at the start of 2015 and looks set to be an important member of the Stamford Bridge set-up for years to come.

MOURINHO'S MEN MATIC

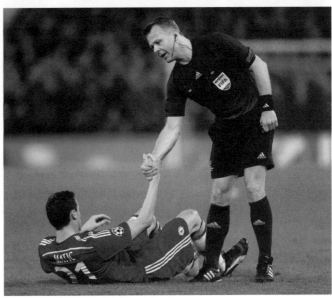

"EVERY PLAYER IN THE SQUAD IS READY TO PLAY AT ANY MOMENT AND THAT'S IMPORTANT FOR US BECAUSE IF WE WANT TO BE CHAMPIONS WE NEED EVERYBODY"

MOURINHO'S MEN MATIC

JOSE SAYS...

"He's a giant. Not for his size, but for the way he plays. The man is a giant. Nemanja has come back a complete player. He breaks things up and has a burst of speed as well when he gets it and dribbles through."

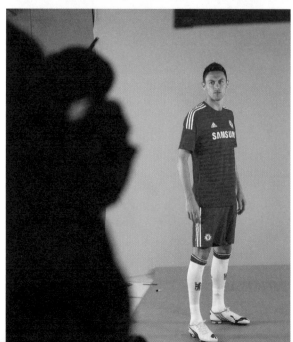

MOURINHO'S MEN MATIC

STATS...

With 35 starts and one appearance from the substitutes' bench, Matic's role in the title success has been crucial, even chipping in with a goal, despite his more defensive holding duties, against Everton last August.

NEMANJA MATIC	
Position: Midfielder	
Date of birth: 01.08.88	
Place of birth: Vrelo-Ub, Serbia	
2014/15 PREMIER LEAGUE	
Appearances	35+1
Minutes	3327
Goals	1
Assists	2

Branislav Ivanovic

Branislav Ivanovic is a big player for this club and he continued to provide big goals.

The ever-dependable Serbian is a world-class defender and his contribution at the other end of the pitch has been crucial in the pursuit of our first Premier League title in five years. Not that his goals come as any great surprise to Chelsea fans.

The defender had scored 25 goals for the club since his arrival from Lokomotiv Moscow until the start of the 2014/15 season, but has netted several more big goals since last August.

He got his account up and running with the goal that sealed a 3-1 win at Burnley in Chelsea's opening Premier League game of the season and scored again two games later as he slammed a shot past Tim Howard to set up a 6-3 win at Everton.

Crucial goals in the Champions League tie at Paris St Germain and the winner in the Capital One Cup semi-final against Liverpool came in a goalscoring spell that saw him net four in six games in January and February.

Both of those league goals saw the Blues earn important points, one of which was a brilliant winner at Aston Villa and the other was Chelsea's only goal in a 1-1 draw with Burnley.

Goals are just the icing on the cake, though, for a player who was a model of consistency and spent most of the season at right-back.

"SEVEN YEARS HERE IS BEAUTIFUL AND I HAVE SPENT THE BEST OF MY CAREER AT CHELSEA. I AM VERY PROUD"

JOSE SAYS...

"I think Branislav will go down as one of
the club's best-ever signings. He came just
after I left [in 2007] and after that he made a
fantastic contribution for this club. He is a great
guy. What he is doing for us is unbelievable."

STATS...

Branislav Ivanovic played every Barclays Premier League game in a defence that kept 17 clean sheets last season. He is a player who rarely seems to pick up injuries and featured in 49 matches overall. Once again, he made a contribution at the other end of the field, scoring six goals, some of which have been vital in our pursuit of honours.

BRANISLAV IVANOVIC	
Position: Defender	
Date of birth: 22.02.84	
Place of birth: Sremska Mitrovica, Serbia	
2014/15 PREMIER LEAGUE	
Appearances	38
Minutes	3652
Goals	4
Assists	10

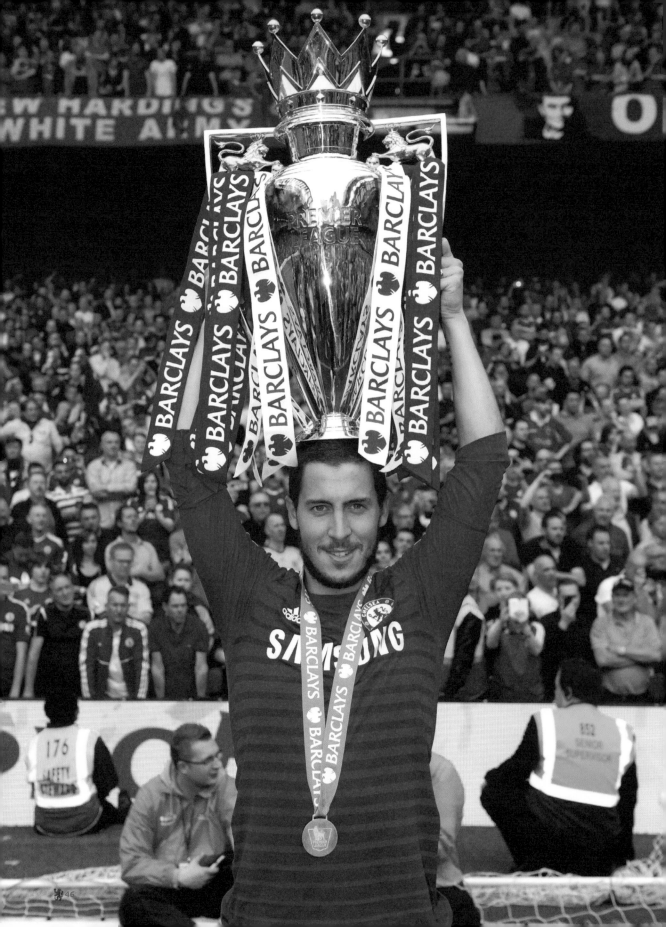

MOURINHO'S MEN

Eden Hazard

What can you say about the performances of Eden Hazard during this title-winning campaign?

Quite simply, he was outstanding from the first minute of the season until the last and was rewarded for his displays with the PFA Players' Player of the Year award, the Football Writers' Association Footballer of the Year trophy, the Chelsea Player of the Year and Barclays Premier League Player of the Year.

Not only is he skilful, creative and a nightmare for defenders to deal with, he is a real goalscoring threat who can pop up all over the pitch and cause major damage to opponents.

And a real feature of his season was his ability to come up with big moments in big games.

He scored goals against Liverpool, Tottenham and Arsenal and the 1-0 home win against Manchester United perhaps best summed up the impact he can have in any game.

In a crucial match where chances were at a premium the Belgian was responsible for the one moment of genuine attacking class.

Oscar received a forward pass from Cesc Fàbregas and the Brazilian brilliantly back-heeled the ball into the path of Hazard who glided forward, composed himself, and then slipped the ball between David de Gea's legs and into the net.

The moment illustrated perfectly why Chelsea became champions as a solid performance provided the foundation for star players further up the pitch to combine beautifully and provide match-winning stardust.

Hazard's undoubted flair is complemented by his mental toughness; a steel which is illustrated when he steps forward to take a penalty.

After years of enjoying Frank Lampard's dead-eye accuracy from the spot, we truly have a successor to the throne in terms of spot-kick expertise.

It is a quality we hope to see much more of in the years to come from a player with the world at his feet.

"I TRY TO PLAY EVERY GAME LIKE IT'S MY LAST. I TRY TO GIVE EVERYTHING. I DON'T WANT TO STOP PLAYING FOOTBALL AND HAVE ANY REGRETS"

JOSE SAYS...

"Eden is a humble kid and he is working a lot for the team and what he is doing for us is very good. Obviously the fans enjoy and respect people that are so stable during the season and do an incredible job for the team, but people like Eden bring the magic and win matches in one action. They have the flair and the artist's touch of the football."

STATS...

Eden Hazard's contribution to the season was massive. The ever-improving Belgian played in every Premier League match, scoring 14 goals. He also played in 14 cup games and picked up a host of individual awards.

EDEN HAZARD

Position: Midfielder
Date of birth: 07.01.91
Place of birth: La Louviere, Belgium

2014/15 PREMIER LEAGUE

Appearances	38
Minutes	3575
Goals	14
Assists	16

3

Filipe Luis

Filipe Luis enjoyed a trophy-laden debut season in England, picking up two winners' medals.

The full-back arrived from Atletico Madrid as part of Chelsea's summer recruitment drive and fitted into José Mourinho's plans as a senior defender the manager knew he could rely on.

A solid, attack-minded player, Filipe Luis was a member of the Atletico side which won La Liga and reached the Champions League final in the 2013/14 season.

Comfortable in possession, he reads the game exceptionally well and possesses the ability to deliver fantastic crosses from wide areas.

After choosing to sign for Chelsea, the Brazilian contributed to left-back duties in the Premier League, and featured in the starting line-up in the majority of Champions League games.

Filipe Luis' first goal for the club came in the Capital One Cup win at Derby County and he played his part in some of the club's biggest wins en route to the title including the 6-3 win at Everton, the 2-1 victory at Liverpool and the 5-0 thrashing of Swansea.

"CHELSEA IS THE BEST CLUB FOR ME TO BE AT TO WIN THE PREMIER LEAGUE. WE HAVE THE BEST COACH AND AN AMAZING SQUAD"

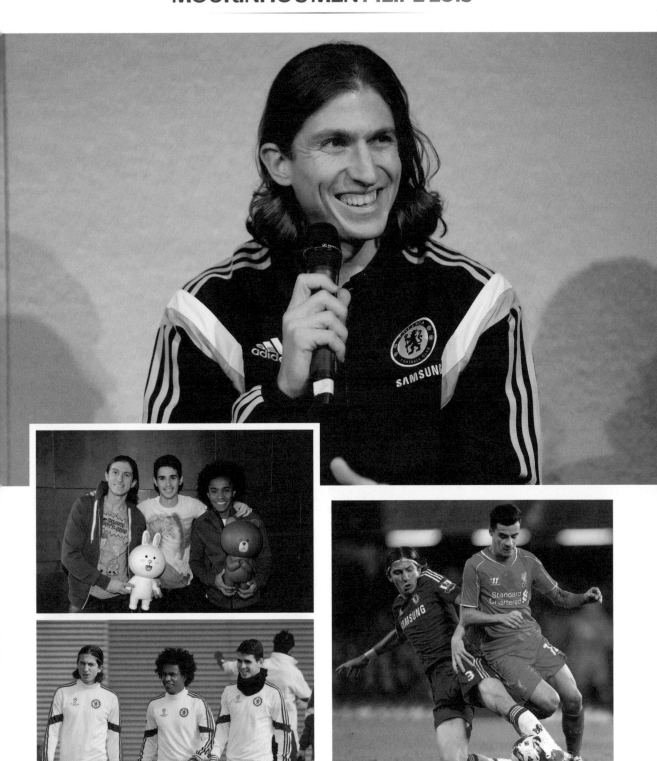

JOSE SAYS...

"It's not easy to come and kick Azpi out of the team because he's such a good player. Our defenders are very young. The second line – Andreas Christensen, Kurt Zouma, Nathan Ake – are very young players so we decided to have an experienced player to have a group of five. He's [Filipe Luis] very stable and experienced."

STATS...

Filipe Luis spent the season vying for the left-back slot with Cesar Azpilicueta. Although the Spaniard played in more Premier League games, his more experienced team-mate still managed 26 appearances overall, 15 of them coming in the league.

FILIPE LUIS

Position: Defender

Date of birth: 09.08.85

Place of birth: Jaragua do Sul, Brazil

2014/15 PREMIER LEAGUE

Appearances	9+6
Minutes	1011
Goals	0
Assists	0

MOURINHO'S MEN

John Mikel Obi

John Mikel Obi added another two medals to his Chelsea collection in 2014/15.

With the Fàbregas-Matic midfield axis firmly established, his first league start came at Newcastle United in early December when the Serbian was suspended. His performance was described by José Mourinho as the best from a player in blue that day.

Mikel then started alongside Matic in four successive victories over Sporting Lisbon – scoring in the 3-1 Champions League win – Hull City,

Derby County (Capital One Cup quarter-final) and Stoke City, before seeing out the month as a starter in the 1-1 draw at Southampton.

The Nigerian midfielder added further appearances in the second half of the league season as he secured a second Premier League title winners' medal, while he made a signficant contribution in the Capital One Cup semi-final first leg at Liverpool, which helped set up the 2-1 aggregate victory and eventual Wembley success – his second win in the competition.

"I HAVE ALWAYS APPRECIATED THE CHELSEA FANS, THEY'VE BEEN AMAZING. THEY'RE ALWAYS THERE TO SUPPORT THE TEAM WHICH JUST SHOWS HOW BRILLIANT THEY ARE"

JOSE SAYS...

"The first time he played [from the start in the Premier League this season] was Newcastle and he was our best player. How can he be our best player if he didn't play in three months? Because he was working every day at the top level. Sad, frustrated, not happy? Maybe. But professional – that's what I expect from the players. It's the concept of helping the team. Everybody has to be ready to sacrifice for the team, to give everything for the team, to think about the team and not to be selfish. This is the way I want a team to be."

STATS...

Mikel made a total of 18 appearances in the Premier League, two Champions League appearances (one goal), started both FA Cup games and was a starter in four of the Capital One Cup ties as he played his part in the Blues' fifth triumph in the competition.

JOHN MIKEL OBI

Position: Midfielder

Date of birth: 22.04.87

Place of birth: Jos, Nigeria

2014/15 PREMIER LEAGUE	
Appearances	6+12
Minutes	773
Goals	0
Assists	1

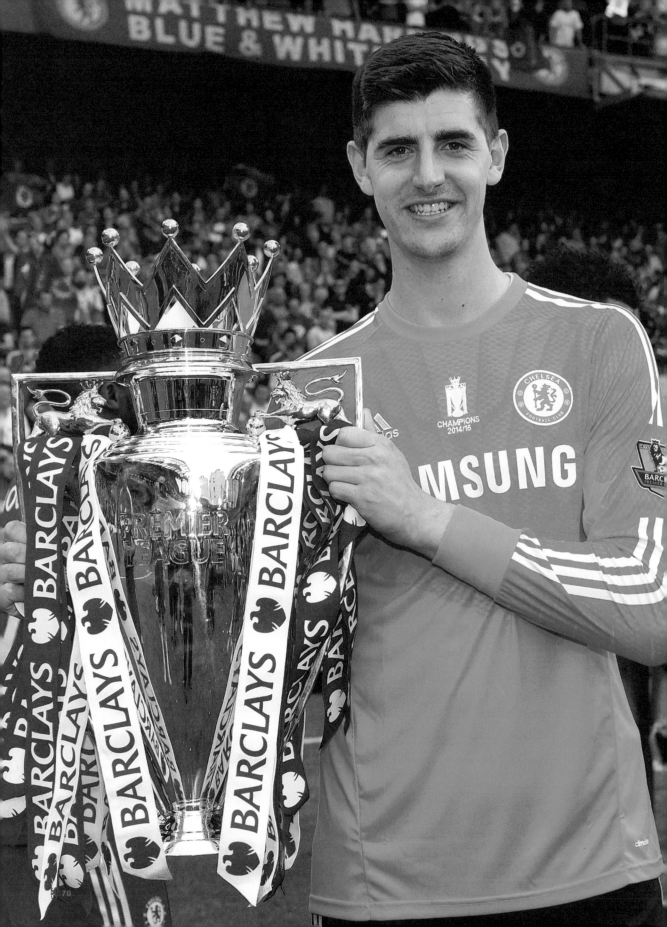

Thibaut Courtois

Having spent three years on loan at Atletico Madrid, picking up a La Liga winners' medal and playing in the Champions League final in the process, José Mourinho brought Thibaut Courtois back to Chelsea as his first-choice keeper for the 2014/15 season.

A towering presence in the Chelsea goal, Courtois has adapted quickly to the demands of English football and was selected ahead of Petr Cech for the opening victory at Burnley.

At Everton in August he produced perhaps the single best save of his Chelsea career to date at Goodison Park, turning compatriot Kevin Mirallas's volley onto the post.

The week before, against Leicester, he had produced a string of wonderful saves to earn his maiden clean sheet for the club.

The Belgian has gone on to establish himself as one of the team's most reliable performers with an ability to stretch his 6'6" frame to make crucial stops and make himself a difficult barrier for any opponent to get past.

Aside from his league performances, Courtois produced some of his best individual displays in the Capital One Cup semi-final against Liverpool where he was named the Man of the Match in both legs.

Despite intense competition within the squad, Courtois has set the platform for what should be a long and successful career for Chelsea.

MOURINHO'S MEN COURTOIS

"NOT ONLY DO WE HAVE THE INDIVIDUALS, BUT WE ALSO HAVE THE TEAM ETHIC; THAT FIGHTING MENTALITY"

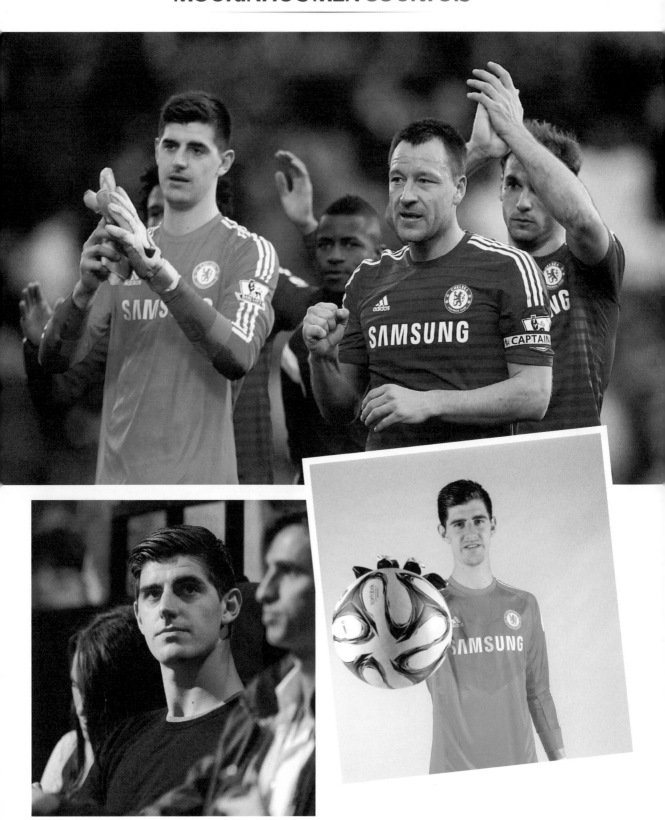

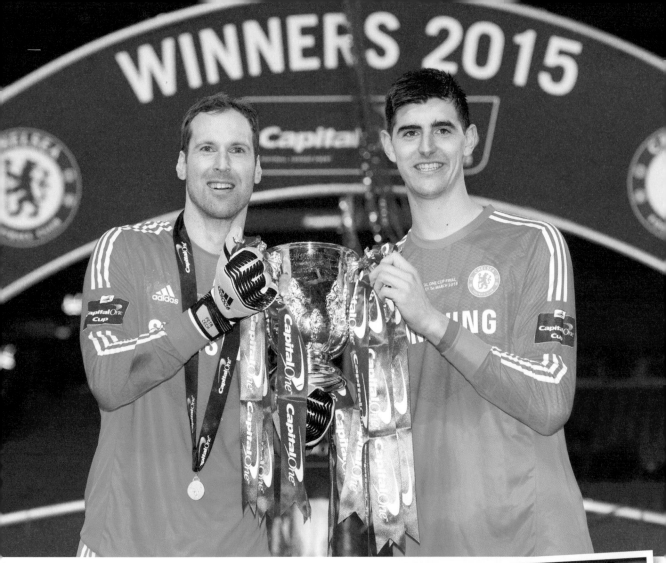

JOSE SAYS...

"We made a decision to make Courtois our first-choice keeper because he is the young one, the future and he is amazing for his age."

STATS...

Courtois was given the nod to play in the majority of Barclays Premier League matches by José Mourinho. He kept 13 clean sheets during his first league season in England and played a big part in the League Cup and Champions League too, making seven cup appearances.

THIBAUT COURTOIS

Position: Goalkeeper
Date of birth: 11.05.92
Place of birth: Bree, Belgium

2014/15 PREMIER LEAGUE	
Appearances	32
Minutes	3009
Clean sheets	13

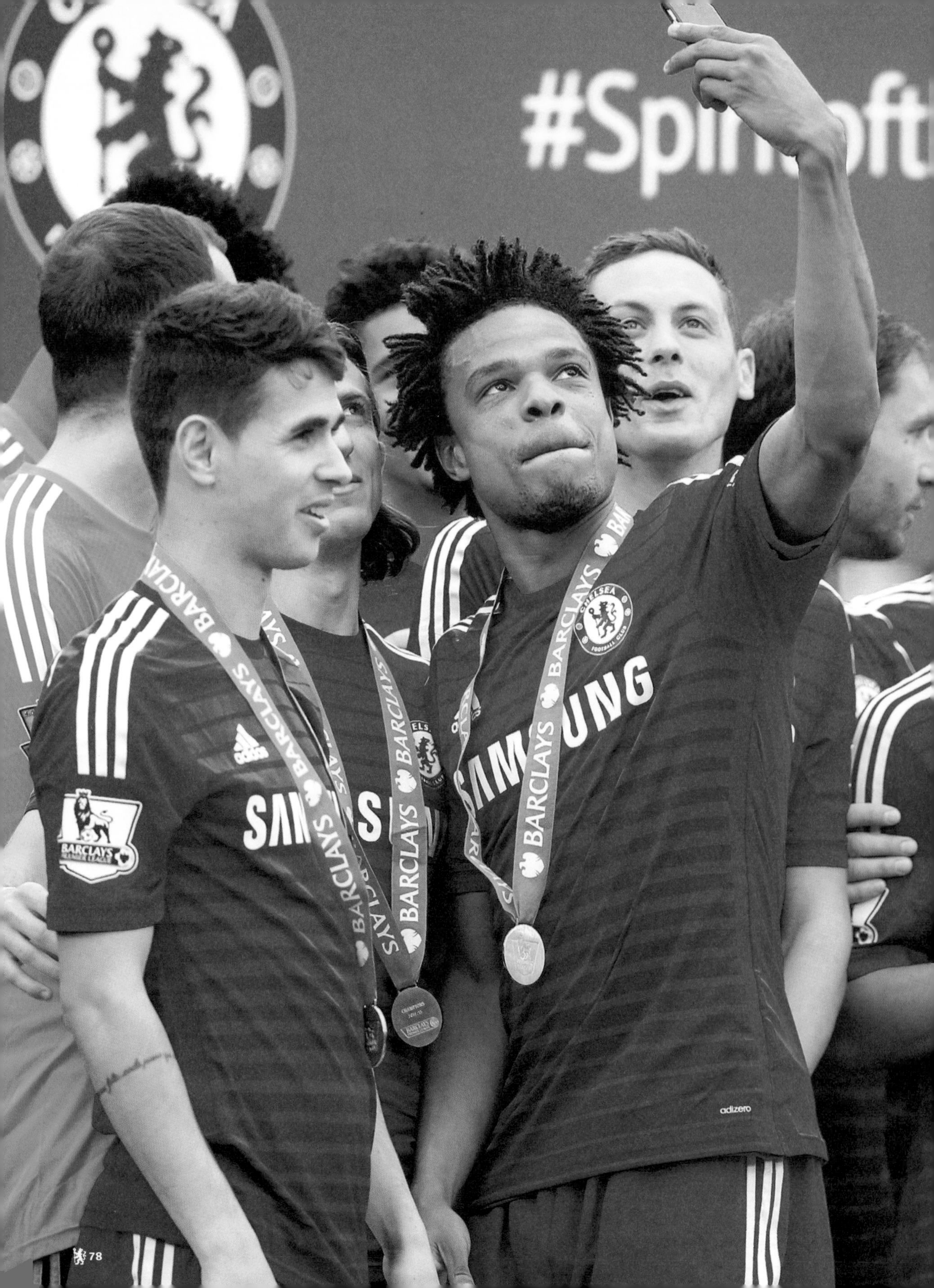
BARCLAYS

Loic Remy

Loic Remy had already shown he had the ability to score goals at Premier League level by the time Chelsea signed him last summer.

He was top scorer at Newcastle while on loan there from QPR in 2013/14 and Remy's Blues career got off to the perfect start, netting on his debut in a 4-2 defeat of Swansea.

The striker continued to provide vital goals, helping to maintain a comfortable gap between Chelsea and second-placed Manchester City thanks to his strike during the 1-1 draw at the Bridge at the end of January.

He also hit the winner away to Hull in March with his first touch after coming off the bench in a 3-2 thriller and claimed the deciding goal in a 2-1 win over Stoke City in April.

Having also opened the scoring in the 6-0 win over Maribor in the Champions League and represented France at the 2014 World Cup finals in Brazil, Remy has shown time and time again that he can perform at the highest level.

And it was left to the striker to round off Chelsea's 2014/15 scoring by netting the club's 72nd and 73rd Premier League goals of the season to seal a 3-1 win against Sunderland in the final game of a triumphant campaign.

MOURINHO'S MEN REMY

"THE PREMIER LEAGUE IS ONE OF THE HARDEST COMPETITIONS TO WIN IN WORLD FOOTBALL. I AM SO PLEASED TO ADD TO MY MEDAL COLLECTION"

JOSE SAYS...

"Every time he plays, scoring or not scoring, he gives us everything he has to give. Sometimes it is movement, sometimes it is defensive contributions, sometimes he is scoring goals."

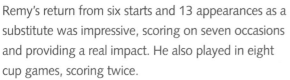

STATS...

Remy's return from six starts and 13 appearances as a substitute was impressive, scoring on seven occasions and providing a real impact. He also played in eight cup games, scoring twice.

LOIC REMY

Position: Forward

Date of birth: 02.01.87

Place of birth: Rillieux-la-Pape, France

2014/15 PREMIER LEAGUE

Appearances	6+13
Minutes	729
Goals	7
Assists	0

MOURINHO'S MEN

Kurt Zouma

For a young man Kurt Zouma has already made a great impact on the Chelsea squad and has played an important part in our title triumph.

Zouma signed for Chelsea from St-Etienne on the final day of the January 2014 transfer window, penning a five-and-a-half year contract, but remained on loan at the French club for the rest of the season.

The 6'3" French Under-21 international then linked up with his new team-mates in the summer of 2014, making his debut against Bolton in the Capital One Cup and marking the occasion by scoring his first goal for the club while playing the full 90 minutes alongside Gary Cahill at centre-back.

While the centre of defence is where he is most comfortable, Zouma can also play at right-back or in a deep midfield position.

He made his Champions League debut when he played the whole of a 6-0 win against Maribor in October, also featuring in the return game two weeks later.

After a handful of Premier League outings before Christmas, Zouma began 2015 on an excellent note, scoring his second goal for the club and our third of the afternoon in a 3-0 FA Cup victory over Watford.

He then played a large part in helping the club secure the Capital One Cup, performing excellently in the semi-final second leg against Liverpool, before taking a defensive midfield role in the final victory over Tottenham Hotspur.

He earned himself many more Premier League minutes in the second half of the season and his strong, assured presence means he's sure to be involved in further Chelsea successes in the future.

"MY DREAM WAS FIRST TO PLAY FOR CHELSEA AND THEN TO WIN ALL THE TITLES I CAN WIN. NOW I AM IN THE DRESSING ROOM WITH A LOT OF VERY GOOD PLAYERS – I AM LIVING THE DREAM"

MOURINHO'S MEN ZOUMA

JOSE SAYS...

"Zouma is now 20 years old and one day he will be 23, 24 and a player with great maturity, probably even with leadership to replace John [Terry] because he is playing more than I expected, more than he expected and more than everyone expected so he is getting experience levels which are very important. He has played in some big matches and it looks like he can cope with it."

STATS...

Even José Mourinho was surprised by the progress Kurt Zouma made in the 2014/15 season. An increasingly important player, he featured in some crucial cup games and made 15 Premier League appearances.

KURT ZOUMA	
Position: Defender	
Date of birth: 27.10.94	
Place of birth: Lyon, France	
2014/15 PREMIER LEAGUE	
Appearances	7+8
Minutes	710
Goals	0
Assists	0

RECLAIMING THE CROWN
STORY OF THE SEASON

STEP 1

Turf Moor, 18.08.14

BURNLEY 1 CHELSEA 3
Arfield 14; Diego Costa 17, Schürrle 21, Ivanovic 34

A devastating display of finishing saw Chelsea recover from the concession of an early goal to see off newly promoted Burnley in our Premier League opener.

The Blues were caught out by a powerful half-volley from Clarets midfielder Scott Arfield, but that merely brought about the best from the boys and we were level just three minutes later courtesy of a debut goal from Diego Costa. The Spaniard fired home after Branislav Ivanovic's low cross came back off the post via a deflection.

Even better was to follow shortly afterwards as a scintillating move saw the Blues going in front via Andre Schürrle, and the victory was virtually assured before the interval when Ivanovic took advantage of slack marking at a corner kick to steer the ball in from close range.

The second-half display was one of complete and utter control from Chelsea, who saw out the victory, and we cruised to the three points with few scares for debutant Thibaut Courtois between the sticks.

STEP 2

Stamford Bridge, 23.08.14

CHELSEA 2 LEICESTER CITY 0
Diego Costa 62, Hazard 77

Second-half goals from Diego Costa and Eden Hazard finally ended Leicester City's brave resistance and ensured the Blues were victorious in our Premier League home opener.

There was little sign of the thrills and spills to come in the second 45 minutes during an opening period in which neither side's attacking players were able to assert any form of dominance.

That all changed after the interval, though, as Oscar hit the post early on and then David Nugent brought an excellent save from Thibaut Courtois. The opening goal wasn't far away, and it was summer signing Diego Costa making it two goals in as many games after superbly chesting down Branislav Ivanovic's cross and stabbing his shot beneath Kasper Schmeichel.

The victory was wrapped up by Eden Hazard, who cut in from the left flank and jinked past several Leicester City defenders before curling a low shot into the back of the net.

This wide-armed celebration became a pleasingly regular feature of Chelsea games in 2014/15 and this one from Diego Costa came after our first goal of the campaign at Burnley

Branislav Ivanovic blasts home as Chelsea made a blistering start to an extraordinary game at Goodison Park which resulted in a 6-3 win

RECLAIMING THE CROWN
STORY OF THE SEASON

STEP 3

Goodison Park, 30.08.14
EVERTON 3 CHELSEA 6
Mirallas 45, Naismith 69, Eto'o 76; Diego Costa 1, 90, Ivanovic 3, Coleman 67 (og), Matic 74, Ramires 77

It was raining goals at Goodison Park as the Blues maintained our 100 per cent start to the season in a nine-goal thriller against Everton.

The tone for an incredible early-evening clash in the North-West was set within three minutes when Chelsea raced into a two-goal lead. Just 35 seconds had elapsed when Diego Costa fired in a low shot before Branislav Ivanovic clinically netted his second goal of the campaign.

Kevin Mirallas' header on the stroke of half-time brought Everton back into it but the Blues' two-goal cushion was restored when Seamus Coleman turned in Eden Hazard's cross.

Steven Naismith's immediate response was followed by a fierce strike by Nemanja Matic, with his first goal for the Blues before Samuel Eto'o marked his debut for the Toffees with a goal. But moments later, Ramires' crisp finish finally ended Everton's resolve and Diego Costa raced clear to beat Howard for a second time and score Chelsea's sixth.

STEP 4

Stamford Bridge, 13.09.14
CHELSEA 4 SWANSEA CITY 2
Diego Costa 45, 56, 67, Remy 81; Terry 11 (og), Shelvey 86

Diego Costa's hat-trick – taking his tally in a Chelsea shirt to seven in just four appearances – and a debut goal from Loic Remy saw off Swansea City at the Bridge in a hugely entertaining game.

The Premier League's two remaining 100 per cent records came face-to-face in west London and the Swans enjoyed the better of the opening exchanges, taking the lead when John Terry put Neil Taylor's cross past his own keeper.

The Blues were level on the stroke of half-time, though, as Diego Costa powered home a header from a corner kick, and the Spaniard added two close-range finishes after the break following good work by Cesc Fàbregas and Ramires respectively.

Our leading scorer made way soon after the hat-trick goal for debutant Remy, who marked the occasion with a smart low finish from Oscar's square pass. Even a late Jonjo Shelvey strike couldn't take the shine off this victory – four wins out of four and a league high of 15 goals scored.

Oscar celebrates opening the scoring against Aston Villa

RECLAIMING THE CROWN
STORY OF THE SEASON

STEP 5

Etihad Stadium, 21.09.14
MANCHESTER CITY 1 CHELSEA 1
Lampard 85; Schürrle 71

Chelsea dropped points in a Premier League fixture for the first time in the 2014/15 campaign after being held to a draw by Manchester City at the Etihad Stadium.

The Blues were 1-0 winners in this fixture the previous season with a controlled counter-attacking display, and the same approach was the order of the day once again as we kept the home side's attacking unit at bay for much of the game.

The second-half dismissal of Pablo Zabaleta looked to have swung the match in our favour, a view that was emphasised when Andre Schürrle applied the finishing touch to a brilliant move which saw the Blues go from one end of the pitch to the other in a matter of seconds.

Diego Costa hit the post soon after when a goal would almost certainly have ended the contest, and it wasn't long until City were on level terms. James Milner was the provider, sending over a cross which Frank Lampard converted to deny his old team-mates the victory.

STEP 6

Stamford Bridge, 27.09.14
CHELSEA 3 ASTON VILLA 0
Oscar 7, Diego Costa 59, Willian 79

It was a game of milestones for Chelsea: our 4,000th league match; 2,000th at home; 5,000th point won, and a 250th game for José Mourinho as Blues boss. Of rather more importance, however, were the three points won against Aston Villa.

The victory never looked in doubt from the moment Oscar benefited from Willian's quick thinking and precise pull-back which teed up the Blues No8.

The early strike put Chelsea in complete control of the contest and that was finally reflected in the scoreline in the second half, starting with an eighth Premier League goal of the season from Diego Costa, who brilliantly headed home Cesar Azpilicueta's cross.

Diego Costa was heavily involved in the third, too, turning Villa's defence inside out before seeing his shot well saved by Brad Guzan. The rebound fell to Willian's feet in the six-yard box and the Brazilian simply could not miss.

Eden Hazard celebrates with the fans after scoring the penalty that put us on the road to a 2-0 victory over Arsenal

RECLAIMING THE CROWN
STORY OF THE SEASON

STEP 7

Stamford Bridge, 05.10.14
CHELSEA 2 ARSENAL 0
Hazard 27 (pen), Diego Costa 78

Chelsea extended our advantage at the top of the Barclays Premier League standings with a comfortable victory over Arsenal.

The Blues suffered an early setback when Thibaut Courtois had to be withdrawn following an accidental collision with Alexis Sanchez, although his replacement was the ever-reliable Petr Cech, who finished the game by extending his club record tally of clean sheets.

The opening goal came courtesy of Eden Hazard from the penalty spot, the Belgian dusting himself down to confidently slot home from 12 yards after being fouled in the area by Laurent Koscielny; it was the only way he could be stopped after a sensational run through the Gunners' rearguard.

Another moment of individual brilliance, this time in the form of a pass, sealed the win in the second half. Cesc Fàbregas, taking on his former club, split the defence with an inch-perfect through-ball; Diego Costa did the rest and a sixth Premier League victory out of seven was secured.

STEP 8

Selhurst Park, 18.10.14
CRYSTAL PALACE 1 CHELSEA 2
Campbell 90; Oscar 6, Fàbregas 51

An action-packed afternoon at Selhurst Park saw Chelsea maintain our five-point lead at the top of the Barclays Premier League thanks to a goal in either half.

Both teams started brightly, Palace evidently buoyed by their surprise win over us in last season's corresponding fixture, but it was the Blues who struck first through Oscar's perfectly placed free-kick which beat Julian Speroni.

A thrilling first half looked to be coming to a conclusion without further drama until the Blues were reduced to 10 men with five minutes remaining. Cesar Azpilicueta received a red card for a late challenge on Mile Jedinak, but the home side's Damien Delaney wasn't far behind as he too was dismissed.

Cesc Fàbregas gave us the perfect start to the second half by scoring his first Premier League goal for Chelsea after a splendid team move, and that proved to be enough despite Fraizer Campbell's late consolation denying John Terry a clean sheet to celebrate his 500th appearance as Blues skipper.

Didier Drogba marked his first start of the season by netting the Blues' goal in a 1-1 draw at Manchester United

STEP 9

Old Trafford, 26.10.14
MANCHESTER UNITED 1 CHELSEA 1
Van Persie 90+4; Drogba 53

Chelsea remained the only undefeated side in the Barclays Premier League, but the Blues were left to rue a last-minute Robin van Persie goal which denied us victory at Old Trafford.

After an entertaining first half, Eden Hazard may have been cursing David de Gea's spectacular save to deny him the opener at the start of the second half after the Belgian had skipped through on goal. However, the breakthrough came from the resulting corner. It's a scene Chelsea fans have seen many times before: a near-post corner met by a bullet header from Didier Drogba, this one coming on his 350th Blues appearance.

That looked to be enough to secure the win, but deep into stoppage time the Red Devils drew level through Van Persie after Branislav Ivanovic was dismissed.

Nevertheless, José Mourinho's men extended our unbeaten record against Manchester United to seven matches – and you have to go back to September 2011 for our last defeat at Old Trafford.

STEP 10

Stamford Bridge, 01.11.14
CHELSEA 2 QUEENS PARK RANGERS 1
Oscar 32, Hazard 75 (pen); Austin 62

Eden Hazard's penalty earned Chelsea a deserved victory over our west London neighbours and maintained both our 100 per cent home record and lead at the top of the Barclays Premier League.

The Blues were able to call upon top scorer Diego Costa after a four-game injury lay-off, but the opening goal came from the right boot of Oscar, which was later named Chelsea's Goal of the Season. And what a strike it was from the Brazilian midfielder, who received a pass from Cesc Fàbregas and bent a superb shot around Robert Green with the outside of his foot.

QPR struggled to assert themselves in the attacking third, but found themselves level just past the hour mark thanks to a neat finish by Charlie Austin. The Blues remained in control, though, and we got our reward with 15 minutes remaining.

The referee pointed to the penalty spot when Hazard was body-checked by Eduardo Vargas and the Belgian sent Green the wrong way from 12 yards to seal a narrow victory.

Diego Costa celebrates slamming in the winner after Chelsea came from behind to clinch a 2-1 win at Anfield

STEP 11

Anfield, 08.11.14
LIVERPOOL 1 CHELSEA 2
Can 9; Cahill 14, Diego Costa 67

Chelsea won at Anfield for the second time in 2014 after goals from Gary Cahill and Diego Costa helped us overcome an early deficit.

There was a stroke of good fortune in the manner of the Reds' ninth-minute opener as Emre Can let fly from distance, with the ball taking a huge deflection off Cahill to leave Thibaut Courtois wrong-footed.

However, we weren't behind for long; Simon Mignolet may have denied John Terry with a superb save, but he couldn't keep out the follow-up from Cahill, which goal-line technology adjudged to have crossed the line.

The Blues seized control of the game from that moment, but the winning goal wasn't forthcoming until midway through the second half. Cesar Azpilicueta was the provider with a driving run down the left and Diego Costa reached double figures for the season with a powerful drilled finish.

The win was our ninth from 11 games in the Premier League.

STEP 12

Stamford Bridge, 22.11.14
CHELSEA 2 WEST BROMWICH ALBION 0
Diego Costa 11, Hazard 25

Early goals from Diego Costa and Eden Hazard secured a comfortable 2-0 victory for the Blues over 10-man West Bromwich Albion.

The first half was packed with, as Ruud Gullit might have said, "sexy football", and it always seemed to be a case of when and not if the home side would open the scoring. It duly came from a reliable source: Diego Costa took his tally for the campaign to 11 with a composed chest and volley finish from Oscar's cross.

Despite Ben Foster's heroics, the keeper could do nothing to keep the in-form Eden Hazard from doubling our advantage. Cesc Fàbregas' quick thinking from a corner kick played in the Belgian for a powerful left-footed shot.

West Brom's task was made all the trickier by the dismissal of Claudio Yacob soon after and the Throstles could have ended up on the receiving end of a hefty scoreline had it not been for Foster's excellence.

Loic Remy sealed another comfortable win over Tottenham at Stamford Bridge

RECLAIMING THE CROWN
STORY OF THE SEASON

STEP 13

Stadium of Light, 29.11.14
SUNDERLAND 0 CHELSEA 0

Chelsea's unbeaten start to the campaign reached 20 games in all competitions, but it was a frustrating evening at the Stadium of Light as we failed to score for the first time in 2014/15.

The opening half was dominated by the Blues and it looked to be only a matter of time before we went in front, but the woodwork denied Willian and Branislav Ivanovic was kept out by Costel Pantilimon.

Gus Poyet's side came out of their shell slightly as the game wore on, though, and it was their turn to curse the goal frame after Santiago Vergini snuck in around the back to strike against the crossbar.

By the conclusion, it was end-to-end stuff and both sides were left to rue a combination of heroic defending and finishing which wasn't of the required level of precision. Somehow, 90 intriguing minutes had elapsed without a goal.

STEP 14

Stamford Bridge, 03.12.14
CHELSEA 3 TOTTENHAM HOTSPUR 0
Hazard 19, Drogba 22, Remy 73

Chelsea's long unbeaten home run against Tottenham Hotspur continued for another season – making it 24 years and counting since our London rivals took all three points at the Bridge, this victory was just about as comfortable as any which preceded it.

Despite the visitors making the brighter start to the game, and even coming as close as hitting the bar through a Harry Kane header, the result was never in doubt after we bagged two goals in three first-half minutes.

Eden Hazard netted the first in sublime fashion, cutting inside and playing a swift one-two with Didier Drogba before rifling a low shot past Hugo Lloris. Drogba went from provider to scorer within a matter of minutes, this time receiving a through ball from Oscar to confidently slot home.

Substitute Loic Remy got in on the action in the second half with another superb goal after replacing Drogba. The Frenchman used his speed to get in behind the Spurs defence and then showed great strength to hold off Jan Vertonghen before side-footing home the third goal our performance deserved.

A second-half strike from Diego Costa helped to ensure Chelsea's 100 per cent league home record continued against Hull City

RECLAIMING THE CROWN
STORY OF THE SEASON

STEP 15

St James' Park, 06.12.14
NEWCASTLE UNITED 2 CHELSEA 1
Cisse 57, 78; Drogba 83

Our 23-match unbeaten run came to an end against Newcastle and the Blues will look back at this game with some frustration after dominating for long spells.

The home side barely had a look-in during the opening 45 minutes, while the Blues twice came close to scoring through Willian, among a host of other chances.

However, the balance of the game shifted in the second period when Newcastle took the lead through Papiss Cisse, who had been on the pitch for only four minutes when he scored from close range.

Cisse doubled their advantage moments after Eden Hazard had hit the post, but the Blues received a lifeline when Steven Taylor was sent off and, from the resulting free-kick, Didier Drogba nodded the ball home.

A fine save from substitute keeper Jak Alnwick denied Diego Costa an equaliser as Chelsea pushed for a late goal.

STEP 16

Stamford Bridge, 13.12.14
CHELSEA 2 HULL CITY 0
Hazard 7, Diego Costa 68

Eden Hazard and Diego Costa scored the goals which got us back to winning ways in the Barclays Premier League and maintained our 100 per cent home record in the top flight.

Against a side set up to frustrate the Blues, it was imperative to score early on to change the dynamic of the game – and that's exactly what we did, courtesy of the in-form Hazard.

The Belgian netted a rare headed goal when he timed his run to perfection to get in between the centre-backs and apply the finishing touch to Oscar's inch-perfect cross.

The task for the visitors became even tougher when Tom Huddlestone was shown a straight red card for a challenge on Filipe Luis, and it was game over soon after thanks to Diego Costa. The Spaniard was back among the goals after being teed up by a delightful through ball from Hazard; the finish was, as we've come to expect, devastating.

Cesc Fàbregas shows
his delight after beating
Asmir Begovic on the way
to victory at Stoke

STEP 17

Britannia Stadium, 22.12.14
STOKE CITY 0 CHELSEA 2
Terry 2, Fàbregas 78

Chelsea secured a valuable three points against Stoke City, coming away from the Britannia Stadium with a 2-0 win.

The Blues controlled the game from the moment we went ahead through an early goal from John Terry. Cesc Fàbregas, who featured in an advanced midfield role as he had done the previous week at Derby, provided the assist from a corner kick; an inviting delivery was emphatically headed home by the skipper to open his Premier League account for the season.

Although there was the occasional period of pressure from the home side, forcing Thibaut Courtois into two impressive saves, Chelsea always looked the more likely to find the net. So it proved late in the second half, Fàbregas smartly controlling an Eden Hazard pass with one touch before bamboozling Asmir Begovic with his next, a scuffed finish into the far corner.

STEP 18

Stamford Bridge, 26.12.14
CHELSEA 2 WEST HAM UNITED 0
Terry 31, Diego Costa 62

A third league win on the bounce was secured with the minimum of fuss as the Blues made light work of West Ham United at Stamford Bridge on Boxing Day.

For the second time in as many games the deadlock was broken by John Terry, who had previously been without a goal in more than 12 months. Unlike at Stoke, the source wasn't his head; on this occasion, his predatory instincts took him inside the six-yard box, where he was perfectly placed to stab home after Diego Costa had headed into his path.

The Blues were dominant against our London rivals, with more than 70 per cent of the possession in the opening half, but the game wasn't made safe until just past the hour mark. Diego Costa got the goal his performance deserved, brilliantly twisting and turning inside the West Ham box before drilling home a clinical finish. The win made it 10 games without defeat against the Hammers at the Bridge and maintained our 100 per cent home record in the Premier League this term.

Eden Hazard's crisp strike earned a point at Southampton

RECLAIMING THE CROWN
STORY OF THE SEASON

STEP 19

St Mary's Stadium, 28.12.14
SOUTHAMPTON 1 CHELSEA 1
Mane 17; Hazard 45+1

The Blues ended 2014 with a three-point lead at the top of the Barclays Premier League despite being held to a 1-1 draw.

Sadio Mane raced through on goal to clip a superb finish over Thibaut Courtois and give the home side an early advantage.

It had been an even start to proceedings until that point, but from then on the Blues took control and in first-half stoppage time Cesc Fàbregas dinked a ball through for Eden Hazard, who beat two defenders in the box to make space for a crisp low strike into the far corner.

Despite spending much of the second period camped in Southampton's half, and the home side being reduced to 10 men late on, we couldn't muster any opportunities to properly test Fraser Forster.

STEP 20

White Hart Lane, 01.01.15
TOTTENHAM HOTSPUR 5 CHELSEA 3
Kane 30, 52, Rose 44, Townsend 45+4 (pen), Chadli 78; Diego Costa 18, Hazard 61, Terry 87

Chelsea fell to our first defeat at White Hart Lane in five years as Spurs took the spoils in an eight-goal thriller.

The Blues took an early lead when Diego Costa stabbed home from close range after being teed up by Oscar, but in the final 15 minutes of the first half the home side netted three times. Harry Kane hit their equaliser with a goal out of nothing and there were further strikes from Danny Rose and Andros Townsend, who scored from the penalty spot.

Kane got his second early in the second half to put Spurs three goals clear, but a wonderful exchange between Cesc Fàbregas and Eden Hazard allowed the latter to reduce the deficit.

However, Nacer Chadli hit a fifth, meaning John Terry's third goal in his last four Premier League appearances was nothing more than a consolation.

A wonderful strike by Oscar put Chelsea 4-0 up before half-time at Swansea

RECLAIMING THE CROWN
STORY OF THE SEASON

STEP 21

Stamford Bridge, 10.01.15
CHELSEA 2 NEWCASTLE UNITED 0
Oscar 43, Diego Costa 59

Goals either side of half-time from Oscar and Diego Costa helped Chelsea to a 2-0 victory over Newcastle United.

The Magpies were the first side to defeat the Blues this term, and they showed a similar performance level in the first half, but Petr Cech and his defenders were able to repel everything that was thrown at them.

The turning point came just before the break. Having won a corner, Willian reacted quickly to the run of Branislav Ivanovic to feed the Serbian right-back, who pulled the ball back for Oscar to side-foot home.

The Blues No8 was heavily involved in our second goal just before the hour mark, showing tremendous awareness and technique to flick a Hazard pass into Diego Costa's path, our Spanish forward duly drilling a low finish past Tim Krul.

STEP 22

Liberty Stadium, 17.01.15
SWANSEA CITY 0 CHELSEA 5
Oscar 1, 36, Diego Costa 20, 34, Schürrle 79

A stunning first-half display helped Chelsea to a 5-0 victory over Swansea at the Liberty Stadium to extend our lead at the top of the Premier League standings.

The scintillating early season away form was back on display from the first whistle, and the game wasn't even one minute old when Oscar rifled us in front after a mistake by Gylfi Sigurdsson.

A lovely passing move preceded another clinical finish from Diego Costa, having been sent clear by Cesc Fàbregas, and the Blues No19 soon had his second of the game, and 17th of the campaign, after another misplaced pass by the Swans put him through on goal.

The result was well and truly safe two minutes later as our goalscoring duo combined for Oscar to smash home a terrific effort, allowing the visitors to cruise through the second half.

The chances continued to come, but there was just one further addition to the scoreline; Branislav Ivanovic's cross was touched in by substitute Andre Schürrle to make it 5-0, our biggest winning margin in the league all season.

Branislav Ivanovic came up with another crucial strike to help the Blues claim all three points at Aston Villa

STEP 23

Stamford Bridge, 31.01.15
CHELSEA 1 MANCHESTER CITY 1
Remy 41; Silva 45

Loic Remy's third Premier League goal for the Blues wasn't enough to defeat Manchester City, but a 1-1 draw maintained our five-point lead over the Citizens.

The opening half was high in intensity. It looked as though the Blues would enter the half-time break with a crucial advantage given to us by Remy, who finished off a beautifully-crafted move. Branislav Ivanovic's floated pass to Eden Hazard was brilliantly volleyed across goal by the Belgian and our No18 simply couldn't miss.

However, City didn't waste any time responding as Sergio Agüero's effort was diverted home by David Silva from close range. Frank Lampard received a hero's welcome from the Bridge crowd when he came on as a late substitute for City, but there was no addition to the scoreline.

STEP 24

Villa Park, 07.02.15
ASTON VILLA 1 CHELSEA 2
Okore 48; Hazard 8, Ivanovic 66

Chelsea moved a further two points clear at the top of the Barclays Premier League table after Branislav Ivanovic's superb half-volley secured a hard-fought victory at Villa Park.

The Blues seized the initiative as early as the eighth minute courtesy of Eden Hazard's 13th goal of the season, which came at the end of a well-worked move. Oscar found Willian inside the box and our No22 spotted the run of Hazard; a perfectly weighted pass was brilliantly swept home by the Belgian.

It was all square shortly after the break, though, as Jores Okore headed home at the back post to end Villa's six-game wait for a goal.

However, it proved to be in vain thanks to the determination of Cesar Azpilicueta and the quality of Ivanovic. Our left-back was the creator, succeeding in picking out a team-mate at the second attempt, and our right-back was the scorer with a controlled half-volley with his so-called weaker foot.

With Manchester City drawing at home to Hull City, the Blues extended our advantage over last season's champions.

RECLAIMING THE CROWN
STORY OF THE SEASON

STEP 25

Stamford Bridge, 11.02.15
CHELSEA 1 EVERTON 0
Willian 89

Chelsea were indebted to a late strike from Willian which secured a hard-fought victory over Everton.

A blistering start by the Blues saw us carve through the Toffees rearguard – which hadn't been breached in the previous three games – on numerous occasions, only for a mixture of near misses and fine goalkeeping from Tim Howard to keep the score level.

The American shot-stopper was playing his first game of 2015, but he displayed great agility to keep out Loic Remy, Nemanja Matic and Willian. At the other end, however, Petr Cech pulled off the save of the evening with a sensational point-blank range block to deny Romelu Lukaku a goal on his return to the Bridge.

It proved to be a pivotal moment in the game. Having seen Branislav Ivanovic's late effort ruled out for offside after he deflected Matic's shot past Howard, Willian ensured we weren't to be denied the victory with a fierce low strike which fizzed home. Just as in the corresponding fixture last term, the Toffees had been undone by a late goal – but it was nothing less than Chelsea deserved.

STEP 26

Stamford Bridge, 21.02.15
CHELSEA 1 BURNLEY 1
Ivanovic 14; Mee 81

A late equaliser for Burnley saw the Blues drop points at Stamford Bridge for only the second time this season, but we were left to rue a series of key decisions which went against us.

Chelsea began the game strongly and went in front through Branislav Ivanovic. The Serbian right-back had been in red-hot form in front of goal, and he wasn't about to pass up the opportunity afforded to him by Eden Hazard's electrifying run.

The lead should have been extended before the break, with two clear penalties denied, and then the game turned on the second-half sending off of Nemanja Matic for his reaction to a challenge from Ashley Barnes, which went unpunished. Burnley took full advantage of their numerical superiority when Ben Mee headed home from a corner kick to earn his side a point.

Eden Hazard headed home a crucial match-winner as the Blues picked up a vital 1-0 victory at West Ham

RECLAIMING THE CROWN
STORY OF THE SEASON

STEP 27

Upton Park, 04.03.15
WEST HAM UNITED 0 CHELSEA 1
Hazard 22

Chelsea followed up our Capital One Cup success against Spurs with an equally important victory over West Ham United which ensured we retained our five-point advantage at the top of the Barclays Premier League table, with a game in hand.

A second London derby in the space of a matter of days was always going to be a test of character for the Blues, but we came through it thanks to a moment of class at one end of the field and typical grit and determination at the other.

Eden Hazard was our match-winner, starting off a counter-attack which ended with the Belgian winger heading home from close range after being picked out by Ramires.

Both sides came close to scoring in the second half, with the marauding Ramires agonisingly hitting the woodwork for the Blues and Thibaut Courtois coming to his side's rescue with a number of excellent saves.

Somehow, the Upton Park crowd were treated to just the one goal – but Chelsea fans didn't mind that one little bit.

STEP 28

Stamford Bridge, 15.03.15
CHELSEA 1 SOUTHAMPTON 1
Diego Costa 11; Tadic 19 (pen)

The Blues were left frustrated by a brilliant goalkeeping display from Fraser Forster which earned Southampton a share of the spoils at Stamford Bridge.

Diego Costa opened the scoring early on in the game when he powerfully headed home Branislav Ivanovic's cross from the right, but the visitors were quickly back on level terms from the penalty spot. Nemanja Matic was adjudged to have brought down Sadio Mane and Dusan Tadic just about managed to beat Thibaut Courtois with his spot-kick.

The Belgian was called upon to make a couple of important saves before the half was out, but the manager's team talk during the interval certainly had the desired effect as we dominated the second half. Indeed, only the excellence of Forster, and a touch of misfortune when Diego Costa's effort found the woodwork instead of the back of the net, denied us the victory our performance after the break had warranted.

A quality finish by Diego Costa was one of several highlights of an entertaining game at Hull City

RECLAIMING THE CROWN
STORY OF THE SEASON

STEP 29

KC Stadium, 22.03.15
HULL CITY 2 CHELSEA 3
Elmohamady 26, Hernandez 28; Hazard 2, Diego Costa 9, Remy 77

Loic Remy came off the substitutes' bench to slot home the late winner which meant Chelsea went into the international break six points clear at the top of the Premier League table.

Our trip to the KC Stadium looked like being one of the most straightforward away days of the campaign thanks to a couple of sensational goals in the opening 10 minutes.

Eden Hazard opened the scoring against the Tigers for the third consecutive game, this time requiring only 80 seconds to jink past a couple of challenges and lash home a left-footed strike from outside the box. Then, just seven minutes later, Diego Costa showed why he is one of the Premier League's best strikers with a superb curling finish with his right foot after being put through by Cesc Fàbregas.

However, the Blues gifted Hull two goals in as many minutes to give the home side parity once again, which is how it remained until the final stages of the game. Remy had been on the field for less then two minutes when he scored the winning goal from Willian's cross to give us a crucial victory in our quest to regain the Premier League title.

STEP 30

Stamford Bridge, 04.04.15
CHELSEA 2 STOKE CITY 1
Hazard 39 (pen), Remy 62; Adam 44

Loic Remy was Chelsea's match-winner for a second straight Premier League game as the Blues continued our march towards the title in a fiercely fought encounter with Stoke City.

The Potters arrived at the Bridge having lost each of their previous visits since winning promotion in 2008, and there was little to suggest that statistic would change as the overworked Asmir Begovic between the sticks kept them in the contest for much of the first half until Eden Hazard stroked home a penalty kick following a foul on Cesc Fàbregas.

That Stoke went in at the break on level terms was entirely down to the audacity of Charlie Adam, who struck a goal of the season contender past Thibaut Courtois from inside his own half.

The Blues wouldn't be denied our victory in the second period, though, despite losing half-time substitute Diego Costa to injury. Remy was the man to provide the crucial breakthrough once again after Begovic's slack throw allowed Willian to intercept before Hazard gave the French striker the easiest of finishes.

The players enjoy the aftermath of a big victory over Manchester United

RECLAIMING THE CROWN
STORY OF THE SEASON

STEP 31

Loftus Road, 12.04.15
QUEENS PARK RANGERS 0 CHELSEA 1
Fàbregas 88

Chelsea chalked up a fifth successive away victory – along with west London bragging rights – after Cesc Fàbregas' late strike at QPR maintained our healthy lead atop the Premier League standings.

Goals have typically been in short supply when these two sides have met at Loftus Road, and this game proved to be no different as scoring opportunities were at a premium throughout a tense 90 minutes.

Thibaut Courtois was called into action on a few occasions to make impressive saves, while at the other end Willian almost caught out Rob Green with a cross which cannoned off the outside of the post.

However, Fàbregas won the game with a superb late intervention as he timed his run into the box to perfection to fire home a low finish from Eden Hazard's set-up. It ensured the 700th game of the Roman Abramovich era ended in the same manner as the first, and so many in between, with the Blues taking all three points.

STEP 32

Stamford Bridge, 18.04.15
CHELSEA 1 MANCHESTER UNITED 0
Hazard 38

Eden Hazard's 18th goal of the season was enough for the Blues to see off the challenge of Manchester United at Stamford Bridge.

The visitors arrived in west London knowing only a win would do – something they hadn't achieved in their previous seven matches against us – and that run now stretched to eight thanks to a wonderful goal by Eden Hazard shortly before the interval.

After John Terry won back possession on the halfway line it took only two passes, the second of which was an exquisite back-heel by Oscar, to send the Belgian clean through and calmly send the ball through the legs of David de Gea into the back of the net.

One goal was all that was needed to seal the three points thanks to a fine defensive display in the second period, with the Red Devils unable to turn their possession into clear-cut chances.

Skipper John Terry enjoys a goalscoring moment after putting Chelsea in the lead at Leicester City's King Power Stadium

RECLAIMING THE CROWN
STORY OF THE SEASON

STEP 33

Emirates Stadium, 26.04.15
ARSENAL 0 CHELSEA 0

Chelsea were prevented from scoring for only the second time in the 2014/15 campaign, but a 0-0 draw at Arsenal kept us on course for the Premier League title and dented our rivals' own hopes in the process.

In a game which saw both sides' defences on top, the Blues could point to several penalty decisions harshly going against us in an entertaining first half when we also created the best chance of the match; Ramires, unfortunately, hit his shot straight at David Ospina after a barnstorming run from Willian.

The home side improved after the half-time interval, but in truth there was little to trouble Thibaut Courtois in the Chelsea goal as he kept a clean sheet for the 12th time in his maiden Premier League season.

The Blues' unbeaten streak against Arsenal now extended to eight matches, while José Mourinho has yet to taste defeat against the Gunners in 13 fixtures across all competitions.

STEP 34

King Power Stadium, 29.04.15
LEICESTER CITY 1 CHELSEA 3
Albrighton 45+3; Drogba 48, Terry 79, Ramires 83

A wonderful second-half comeback by the Blues put José Mourinho's side within touching distance of the Barclays Premier League title.

Marc Albrighton's well-taken goal on the stroke of half-time had the King Power Stadium rocking, but the feel-good factor among the rejuvenated Foxes proved to be short-lived as Chelsea fired in three goals after the break.

Didier Drogba equalised early in the second period with a clinical finish from Branislav Ivanovic's pull-back and it was only a matter of time before the Blues would take the lead.

The goal duly came with a little over 10 minutes remaining as captain John Terry flicked the ball home from close range after Gary Cahill had headed a Cesc Fàbregas corner into his path, and Ramires put the seal on the victory with a superb side-footed finish with his weaker left foot.

The championship equation became very simple: win the next match against Crystal Palace and the title would be ours.

127

The players enjoy the sweet feeling of knowing they are the champions after victory over Crystal Palace

RECLAIMING THE CROWN
STORY OF THE SEASON

STEP 35

Stamford Bridge, 03.05.15
CHELSEA 1 CRYSTAL PALACE 0
Hazard 45

Chelsea clinched our fourth Barclays Premier League title with three games to spare thanks to a first-half winner from Eden Hazard.

A sunny afternoon in west London had all the makings of being a frustrating one for the Blues as the visitors set up shop early on to defend deep and try to punish us on the counter-attack. The plan did not, however, account for a moment of magic from the newly-crowned PFA Player of the Year.

With half-time approaching, Hazard seized the initiative and, after a neat one-two with Willian, the Belgian was impeded in the area. Julian Speroni tried his best to be the party pooper as he kept out the spot-kick, but Hazard was on hand to head home the rebound to put us in front.

A solitary goal proved to be enough and, despite a brief spell of Palace pressure with the final whistle looming, Stamford Bridge erupted in celebration as the Blues clinched a first Premier League title since 2010.

STEP 36

Stamford Bridge, 10.05.15
CHELSEA 1 LIVERPOOL 1
Terry 5; Gerrard 44

Chelsea maintained our unbeaten home record in this season's Barclays Premier League after a record-setting goal by John Terry was cancelled out by Steven Gerrard.

It was a much-changed starting XI from the side which clinched the title against Crystal Palace, including a full debut for Academy graduate Ruben Loftus-Cheek, and they were welcomed on to the pitch by a guard of honour formed by the visitors for the new champions.

Despite the changes, the Blues started strongly and Terry headed in Cesc Fàbregas' corner to become the highest-scoring defender in Premier League history.

It was a set-piece at the other end which proved to be our undoing, though, as the Reds equalised shortly before the half-time interval through Gerrard's header at the back post – a rare goal for the Liverpool skipper against the Blues in what is likely to be his final appearance at Stamford Bridge.

The visitors arguably shaded the second half, but neither side could find that elusive winning goal.

Didier Drogba is carried from the pitch on his last appearance for the club against Sunderland

RECLAIMING THE CROWN
STORY OF THE SEASON

STEP 37

The Hawthorns, 18.05.15
WEST BROMWICH ALBION 3 CHELSEA 0
Berahino 9, 47 (pen), Brunt 60

Chelsea slipped to only our third Premier League defeat of the season, and first since New Year's Day, as West Bromwich Albion ran out 3-0 victors at The Hawthorns.

The Throstles seized the advantage early on through an opportunistic strike from Saido Berahino and the Blues' hopes of a positive result took another hit just before the half-hour mark when Cesc Fàbregas saw red.

Berahino netted his second of the game early in the second half from the penalty spot after being felled by John Terry, but the Blues almost halved the deficit when Loic Remy drilled in a left-footed shot which came back off the post. Instead, Chris Brunt added to the home side's advantage with a fierce strike which caught out Thibaut Courtois.

Despite the scoreline and our 16-match unbeaten run in the Premier League coming to an end, the travelling supporters were in fine voice as the game reached its conclusion.

STEP 38

Stamford Bridge, 24.05.15
CHELSEA 3 SUNDERLAND 1
Diego Costa 37 (pen), Remy 70, 88; Fletcher 26

The Blues ended the 2014/15 campaign exactly as we started it, coming from behind to turn a one-goal deficit into a 3-1 victory on the day the Barclays Premier League trophy was presented to José Mourinho's dominant side.

Didier Drogba was handed the captain's armband for his final Chelsea appearance, but his planned departure after 30 minutes was preceded by Sunderland taking the lead through Steven Fletcher.

It proved to be short-lived, however, as substitute Diego Costa drilled home from the penalty spot after Juan Cuadrado had been brought down in the box.

Another substitute, Loic Remy, ensured we could enjoy the title celebrations with a victory as he scored two late goals. The first was a superb finish after he was teed up by Eden Hazard at the end of a typically mazy run from the Belgian, while the second owed much to the good work of Nemanja Matic.

Even so, this was a day when the result had little relevance – it was all about the trophy presentation and the chance to say goodbye to a Blues legend.

Diego Costa

Signed from Spanish champions Atletico Madrid in July 2014, the 25-year-old centre-forward made a huge impact in his first season at Stamford Bridge, helping fire the Blues to league and cup success.

But for injuries, the striker's goalscoring numbers could have been even more impressive.

The focal point of José Mourinho's 4-2-3-1 formation, the Spain international fired seven goals in his first four games, displaying the full array of finishing prowess in his armoury. His tally included a double in a remarkable 6-3 triumph at Everton and his first hat-trick in English football in a 4-2 defeat of Swansea City.

His and the team's good form continued into October and November, despite the striker suffering from a hamstring problem, with a memorable lob against Arsenal at the Bridge and the winner against Liverpool among the pick of his extensive bunch.

Over the festive period he reached 14 league goals, with a goal apiece against London rivals West Ham and Tottenham, a clinical finish against the Hammers on Boxing Day being a highlight.

His penchant for playing Swansea also continued in the return match in Wales in January, scoring twice in a 5-0 victory, and in his first appearance at Wembley for the club, his goal secured the 2-0 Capital One Cup final win over Tottenham in March.

He hit two goals in two games later that month, against Southampton and Hull City, before an injury recurrence meant he had no further involvement until the last two games of the season.

Typically, he ended on a high note, netting from the penalty spot on a celebratory occasion as Chelsea wrapped up the season with a 3-1 win against Sunderland.

There can be little doubt that Diego Costa found Premier League football to his liking.

"WINNING TITLES. THAT'S EXACTLY WHAT A GOOD SEASON MEANS FOR A CLUB LIKE THIS. BUT WE MUST KEEP ON IMPROVING, WHICH IS WHAT THE MANAGER DEMANDS"

JOSE SAYS...

"The team was built in a way where
we were waiting for a certain type of
striker. I think now everybody knows
Chelsea did the right thing waiting for
him. Chelsea did well by waiting and
waiting for the right one."

STATS...

Diego Costa's first season in English football was a triumph, his 20 league goals coming in 24 starts, plus two substitute appearances. He followed that up with seven appearances in the Champions League, one in the FA Cup and three in the Capital One Cup – his solitary cup goal coming at Wembley. Internationally he also scored his first goal for Spain in a 4-0 European Championships 2016 qualifying victory over Luxembourg.

DIEGO COSTA	
Position: Forward	
Date of birth: 07.10.88	
Place of birth: Lagarto, Brazil	
2014/15 PREMIER LEAGUE	
Appearances	24+2
Minutes	2167
Goals	20
Assists	4

Cesar Azpilicueta

Cesar Azpilicueta has continued to enhance his reputation with another consistent year wearing the blue of Chelsea.

The Spaniard, who is a favourite with the fans, had a strong season in 2013/14 and was José Mourinho's first-choice left-back for the 2014/15 campaign in what was a settled back four.

Many expected the arrival of a top-quality full-back in Filipe Luis in the summer of 2014 to have put pressure on Azpilicueta for his position. If it did, it only brought the best out of him.

Azpilicueta's season was characterised by a focus on his defending, but he was eager to raid down the wing when opportunities presented themselves to help launch attacks.

While he didn't get on the scoresheet himself during the season – he left Branislav Ivanovic to take the role of 'goalscoring full-back' – he is as comfortable in the opponents' third of the pitch as he is his own team's defensive areas.

No moment summed up his attacking value more than the part he played in setting up Diego Costa's winner against Liverpool at Anfield in November. He scurried past Philippe Coutinho on the left wing then curled a cross into the six-yard box which keeper Simon Mignolet couldn't deal with, allowing Diego Costa to smash the ball in.

If Azpilicueta continues to perform at his current level he could nail down his position for years to come and become a Chelsea legend.

"EVERY PLAYER WANTS TO WIN THE TITLE. WHEN I CAME HERE MY TARGET WAS TO TRY TO WIN AS MUCH AS I COULD. TROPHIES ARE WHAT I WANT"

JOSE SAYS...

"Azpilicueta is the kind of player I like a lot. I think a team with 11 Azpilicuetas probably could win the Champions League because football is not just about the pure talent. Football is also about character and personality and Azpilicueta has all those traces of a winning personality."

STATS...

Cesar Azpilicueta had a consistent season, only missing nine league games through injury, suspension or when Filipe Luis filled in. In all, he racked up 40 appearances, 29 of them coming in the Premier League, and he passed the milestone of his 100th Chelsea game.

CESAR AZPILICUETA

Position: Defender
Date of birth: 28.08.89
Place of birth: Pamplona, Spain

2014/15 PREMIER LEAGUE

Appearances	29
Minutes	2651
Goals	0
Assists	4

Petr Cech

Competition for places in any squad is essential if you want to battle for the top honours.

There can be no doubt that Chelsea have several top-class players in a number of positions but no manager in Europe had stronger goalkeeping options than José Mourinho in 2014/15.

Petr Cech spent large chunks of the season on the bench but that was no indication of a decline in quality or his diminishing importance to Chelsea's pursuit of honours. It was purely down to the rise to prominence of Thibaut Courtois and the pair drove each other on to deliver incredible consistency.

If one goalkeeper had to miss a game, the other would come in and provide a seamless transition which meant that Chelsea's back four, in any given match, knew they had a reliable man behind them.

So while Courtois may have started the season as the manager's first choice for Premier League matches, in the first five games where Cech played instead of the Belgian, Chelsea kept five clean sheets.

Cech played in the big win at Leicester in April and the final game of the season against Sunderland.

Cech also featured in a series of domestic and European cup matches and helped the team to a clean sheet in the Capital One Cup final.

Indeed, Cech is our all-time record clean sheet holder and our foreign player with the most appearances of all time.

It all backed up the manager's view that he was lucky enough to have two of the best goalkeepers in the world.

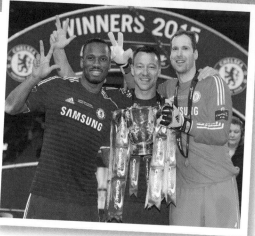

"YOU NEED TO TRY EVERY GAME TO BE READY AND BE COMPETITIVE AND TO BE SURE AT THE END OF THE SEASON YOU HAVE THE MOST POINTS POSSIBLE"

JOSE SAYS...

"Petr Cech is not a player, he's an institution. Ten years in goal going through everything; great moments, sad moments, almost dying on the pitch."

STATS...

Petr Cech managed seven appearances and five clean sheets in the league in 2014/15. The Czech, who has more clean sheets for Chelsea than any other keeper in history, also picked up two more winners' medals to bring his haul for the club to 13 major titles.

PETR CECH	
Position: Goalkeeper	
Date of birth: 20.05.82	
Place of birth: Plzen, Czech Republic	
2014/15 PREMIER LEAGUE	
Appearances	6+1
Minutes	645
Clean sheets	4+1

Willian

Willian was a regular in the Blues' title-winning side in only his second season in English football, being used mainly as one of the three attacking midfielders behind the striker.

The Brazilian's tenacity with and without the ball was in evidence throughout, as was his interchange with fellow attack-minded players Oscar, Eden Hazard and Cesc Fàbregas.

Willian scored his first goal of the season against Aston Villa and by the midway point of the campaign he had followed that up with the second goal against Schalke in the 5-0 Champions League victory in Germany, and opened the scoring against Watford in the FA Cup.

The midfielder's late winner thwarted a determined Everton side at the Bridge, to extend the Blues' lead at the top of the table to seven points in mid-February, a crucial moment as the club maintained its stranglehold on the title race.

His contribution to Chelsea's attacking play and immense workrate was well appreciated by the fans, his team-mates and his manager.

"WHEN I CAME HERE I DREAMED ABOUT PLAYING IN FINALS AND HAVING THE OPPORTUNITY TO WIN TROPHIES. I'M LIVING OUT MY DREAM"

JOSE SAYS...

"Willian is the kind of player that without scoring goals he gives so much to the team. He creates, he always has a good dynamic. When the team lose the ball he's probably the first defender because he reacts in a very effective way, he presses immediately and recovers balls. Willian always gives us a performance."

MOURINHO'S MEN WILLIAN

STATS...

Willian missed only two Premier League games, scoring two goals and assisting six other strikes. He added a further two goals – in the Champions League and FA Cup – and appeared in seven European games, as well as several domestic cup games.

WILLIAN

Position: Midfielder

Date of birth: 09.08.88

Place of birth: Ribeirao Pires, Brazil

2014/15 PREMIER LEAGUE

Appearances	28+8
Minutes	2526
Goals	2
Assists	6

Gary Cahill

Gary Cahill has continued to become one of the most important members of Chelsea's squad.

An almost constant fixture of the first-team line-up, the England international helps to provide a stable base for the team alongside John Terry at centre-back, allowing the attacking talents further up the field to go and express themselves.

Cahill was a key part of a back four which hardly changed in the first half of the season and provided a platform for a championship challenge.

A personal highlight in those opening months came in the form of his strike at Anfield in November which crept over the line during the 2-1 win against Liverpool. The goal came moments after the home side had taken the lead and allowed Diego Costa to go on and grab a crucial winner.

Cahill went on to add a few more goals in the cup competitions but it is at the back where his most valuable contributions were made and his reliability and strength are vital assets for a manager who always wants his team to be hard to beat.

Cahill added his first Premier League medal to the Champions League, Europa League, FA Cup and League Cup honours he has already won in three-and-a-half years as a Chelsea player.

It is no wonder he has become so important to club and country.

MOURINHO'S MEN CAHILL

"YOU WORK VERY HARD ALL SEASON AND THE PREMIER LEAGUE TROPHY IS THE PRIZE"

JOSE SAYS...

"He is not the captain here because we made the decision that John [Terry] is the captain for many, many years. But can he be a captain, do I feel he has the captain's profile? Yes."

STATS...

Gary Cahill was a virtual ever-present in Chelsea's charge to the title. He played 36 games, helping the club to keep 17 clean sheets in the league, and chipped in with a goal. He also played nine games for England during the 2014/15 campaign.

GARY CAHILL	
Position: Defender	
Date of birth: 19.12.85	
Place of birth: Sheffield	
2014/15 PREMIER LEAGUE	
Appearances	33+3
Minutes	3199
Goals	1
Assists	0

MOURINHO'S MEN

Didier Drogba

The old saying is that you can get too much of a good thing, but when it comes to Didier Drogba that certainly isn't the case.

When he left the club in 2012 after spearheading the Champions League final victory over Bayern Munich he clearly hadn't had his fill of Chelsea, and the Stamford Bridge fans certainly hadn't seen enough of him.

His combination of power, ability and top-class finishing had made him a hero in west London and a fearsome prospect for any opponent in the Premier League and Europe to handle during his initial eight-year spell with the club.

So in July 2014 the announcement came that Drogba had signed a one-year deal to return to the club where he'd made himself a legend having spent time away playing in China and Turkey.

Drogba was one third of a trio of signings in the forward department that transformed our attacking unit and gave José Mourinho a variety of options to choose from up front.

And though the Ivorian would spend much of his comeback season as back-up to Diego Costa and Loic Remy, he still had the hunger and skills to make a huge impact when called upon.

He made his return as a late substitute in our 3-1 win at Burnley, and in our first Stamford Bridge game of the season, against Leicester City, the striker was brought on to a hero's welcome.

Drogba scored his first league goal since returning with a header against Manchester United at Old Trafford and would net further Premier League goals against Tottenham Hotspur, Newcastle United and Leicester City.

He was made captain for the final game of the season against Sunderland and was famously carried off the pitch by his team-mates in the first half, having cemented his place in the hearts of Chelsea fans.

MOURINHO'S MEN DROGBA

"I'M NOT HERE TO BREAK RECORDS, I JUST WANT TO WIN TROPHIES. FIVE YEARS IS A LONG TIME NOT TO WIN THE PREMIER LEAGUE"

MOURINHO'S MEN DROGBA

JOSE SAYS...

"If I was a young player and I played with this guy on my side, what more could I wish for? For the kids it must be a privilege and they have to learn by example – the example the older guys give. We want to win matches and win titles and Didier is one of the best strikers in Europe. He is still very adapted to the needs of the Premier League."

MOURINHO'S MEN DROGBA

STATS...

For a man who was brought back as a squad player and mentor for the youngsters, Didier Drogba made a lot of appearances for Chelsea in 2014/15. In all, he played 28 Premier League games, scoring four goals, and was the oldest goalscorer in the Premier League during the campaign.

DIDIER DROGBA	
Position: Forward	
Date of birth: 11.03.78	
Place of birth: Abidjan, Ivory Coast	
2014/15 PREMIER LEAGUE	
Appearances	8+20
Minutes	980
Goals	4
Assists	1

MOURINHO'S MEN

Ramires

Ramires displayed the ability and will to win which have made him an integral part of the team since he joined Chelsea in August 2010, even though his season was hampered by injury and illness.

The 2014/15 campaign began promisingly for the Brazilian, scoring in his first start of the season away to Everton.

At Manchester City in September, he suffered a groin injury which kept him out of action until early November, when he netted against Schalke in the Champions League in Germany.

After working his way back to full fitness, Ramires started to feature in some of the biggest games of the season, including the Capital One Cup semi-final win over Liverpool at the Bridge and the Champions League Round of 16 tie against Paris St-Germain.

He also started the Capital One Cup final victory against Tottenham at Wembley.

Unfortunately, he fell ill before the title-clinching win over Crystal Palace in May, ending his season prematurely, but he still managed 23 league appearances in a title-winning campaign.

"WHEN A TEAM STARTS A COMPETITION WITH THE FRAME OF MIND THAT YOU WANT TO WIN THE TROPHY, IT'S A PROUD MOMENT WHEN YOU DO IT"

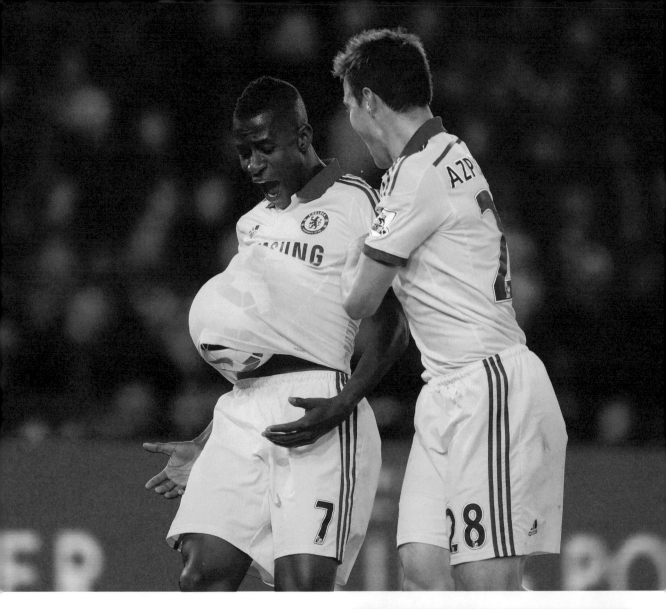

JOSE SAYS...

"Ramires is a champion: a fantastic professional.
Step by step, he works hard and is always available
for the team."

STATS...

With injuries taking their toll in the 2014/15 campaign, Ramires made 23 appearances in the league – with 12 of those coming from the bench. He was still busy when on the pitch, though, providing two league goals, two assists and plenty of energy. He also made 11 appearances in cup competitions, scoring two further goals.

RAMIRES	
Position: Midfielder	
Date of birth: 24.03.87	
Place of birth: Barra do Pirai, Brazil	
2014/15 PREMIER LEAGUE	
Appearances	11+12
Minutes	1204
Goals	2
Assists	2

BARCLAYS
PREMIER LEAGUE
CHELSEA FOOTBALL CLUB
BARCLAYS PREMIER LEAGUE
adizero

Juan Cuadrado

Juan Cuadrado signed for the Blues from Fiorentina on 2 February 2015, putting pen to paper on a four-and-a-half-year contract.

Upon signing, the 26-year-old said: "I am very happy and thankful for this opportunity I've been given. This is a great club and honestly it is like a dream to join the Chelsea family and to know that the manager believes in me. I'm happy."

Cuadrado immediately joined the first-team fold and made his Premier League debut during the 2-1 win at Aston Villa, adding a first start in the 1-0 win over Everton.

The Colombian went on to feature in several more Premier League games, the Champions League and came off the bench to play his part in the Capital One Cup final victory over Tottenham Hotspur.

The attacking midfielder moved to Stamford Bridge after five-and-a-half years in Italy, first with Udinese before switching to Fiorentina in 2012 after a loan spell at Lecce.

Cuadrado plays predominantly behind a striker, but he is also comfortable on either flank.

Pacy and agile, he is a purposeful attacking threat with an eye for the spectacular.

MOURINHO'S MEN CUADRADO

"WE ARE A BIG CLUB SO WE WANT TO WIN IMPORTANT THINGS. PLAYING FOR THIS TEAM THE LEAGUE CHAMPIONSHIP IS THE MOST IMPORTANT THING"

JOSE SAYS...

"It's normal, step by step, to be integrated. He
needs time. I know Italy and I know the difference
between Italy and England. His formation, his
development, his experience – everything was
in Italy. I wasn't expecting him to come on to
the pitch in his first game against Aston Villa and
destroy them. Stability, time, integration – I think
we will see the best Cuadrado next year."

MOURINHO'S MEN CUADRADO

STATS...

It was a few months of settling in for Juan Cuadrado. Since arriving halfway through the season he featured in 12 league games (14 in all competitions) for Chelsea from February through to May, picking up two winners' medals in the process!

JUAN CUADRADO

Position: Midfielder

Date of birth: 26.05.88

Place of birth: Necoclí, Colombia

2014/15 PREMIER LEAGUE

Appearances	4+8
Minutes	347
Goals	0
Assists	1

Cesc Fàbregas

When Chelsea signed Cesc Fàbregas in the summer of 2014 they knew they were guaranteed to be getting a top-quality Premier League performer, but even José Mourinho must have been surprised by just how quickly the Spaniard re-adapted to the demands of English football.

Football fans in this country are well aware of the talents of the Spanish midfielder, having seen him develop at Arsenal and from a distance during his three seasons at Barcelona, yet his impact when he moved to west London was immediate and impressive.

A versatile, technically-gifted midfielder, Fàbregas has acquired a wealth of experience from playing in two of the strongest leagues in Europe and representing the most successful Spanish international side of all time.

Fàbregas' time at Stamford Bridge got off to a flyer with two assists on his debut away at Burnley. By the end of November he had plenty more to his name, as well as two goals, with a host of impressive midfield performances alongside Nemanja Matic helping the Blues reach the Premier League summit.

The assists kept flowing and he ended the season as the league's most prolific assist-maker.

Fàbregas also played the full 90 minutes as we overcame Tottenham at Wembley in the Capital One Cup final and supplied the pass which led to the second goal in our 2-0 victory. It was the Spaniard's first medal as a Chelsea player. It wasn't his last.

By the time the season was over our number four had claimed a Premier League winners' medal and confirmed his status as one of the division's top midfielders.

"I LOOKED AT ALL THE OFFERS I HAD AND AFTER SPEAKING TO THE COACH I THOUGHT CHELSEA WAS THE BEST DECISION. MY AMBITIONS? MY AMBITIONS WERE TO WIN ABSOLUTELY EVERYTHING"

JOSE SAYS...

"He's playing so well for us and what I like especially – more than his quality – is the person. He's a professional. A big player like him, a world champion, comes to play in a Capital One Cup match and plays so well – this is the kind of attitude I want from my players."

STATS...

Cesc Fàbregas was one of the main thrusts behind this title win, providing quality and craft in the midfield engine room. His outstanding stat this season has come in the 'assists' column which shows that he played a crucial part in setting up 24 goals in his 34 Premier League appearances. He's also chipped in with three goals for good measure.

CESC FABREGAS	
Position: Midfielder	
Date of birth: 04.05.87	
Place of birth: Arenys de Mar, Spain	
2014/15 PREMIER LEAGUE	
Appearances	33+1
Minutes	3062
Goals	3
Assists	24

Mohamed Salah

Attacking midfielder Mohamed Salah made eight appearances for the club this season, before spending the second half of the campaign on loan at Fiorentina.

Having signed for the club in January 2014, the Egyptian showed plenty of promise in his first few months as a Chelsea player and this season he made eight appearances. Of those games he played (three in the league), Chelsea won all of the first six.

He scored nine goals during a successful spell in Italy, the highlight being the two goals he scored in a 2-1 win at Juventus in the Coppa Italia.

MOHAMED SALAH	
Position: Midfielder	
Date of birth: 15.06.92	
Place of birth: Basuon, Egypt	
2014/15 PREMIER LEAGUE	
Appearances	0+3
Minutes	45
Goals	0
Assists	0

Andre Schürrle

He may have moved on to pastures new, but Andre Schürrle's contribution to our success in 2014/15 won't be forgotten.

The goalscoring midfielder, fresh from a World Cup-winning campaign with Germany, made a great start to the season by scoring a wonderful goal in our Premier League opener at Burnley.

He scored two more league goals, one of them a crucial strike against Manchester City and the other in his final game as a Chelsea player in the 5-0 win at Swansea City.

He also chipped in with goals against Sporting Lisbon in the Champions League and Derby County in the Capital One Cup.

He left to join Wolfsburg at the end of the January transfer window.

ANDRE SCHURRLE	
Position: Midfielder	
Date of birth: 06.11.90	
Place of birth: Ludwigshafen, Germany	
2014/15 PREMIER LEAGUE	
Appearances	5+9
Minutes	479
Goals	3
Assists	0

MOURINHO'S MEN

Ruben Loftus-Cheek

This has been a big season for Ruben Loftus-Cheek.

José Mourinho handed the midfielder a first-team debut in a Champions League game against Sporting Lisbon in December 2014, and he had his first taste of Premier League action when he came on as a late substitute in our 1-1 draw against Manchester City at the end of January.

In February, Loftus-Cheek was elevated permanently into the first-team squad, although the midfielder was still part of the Under-19 side which won the UEFA Youth League courtesy of a 3-2 final victory over Shakhtar Donetsk in April 2015.

The following month he made his maiden start for the first-team, playing an hour against Liverpool at Stamford Bridge, and backed that up with another start against West Bromwich Albion the following week.

The future looks bright for a youngster who, at 19, can already claim to have played a part in a title-winning campaign.

RUBEN LOFTUS-CHEEK

Position: Midfielder

Date of birth: 20.01.96

Place of birth: Lewisham

2014/15 PREMIER LEAGUE

Appearances	2+1
Minutes	138
Goals	0
Assists	0

Isaiah Brown

Eighteen-year-old Isaiah Brown will always remember the 2014/15 season. It was the year the exciting attacking player made his Chelsea first-team debut.

Brown was included in José Mourinho's squad which headed to Europe for a two-week training camp ahead of the 2014/15 season and was named on the substitutes' bench for our Capital One Cup tie away at Shrewsbury and then again for our Premier League game against Manchester City at the end of January.

In February 2015 he was officially promoted to the first-team squad before his debut arrived, coming on as a substitute for Loic Remy against West Bromwich Albion at The Hawthorns.

Brown has also been busy performing away from the first-team spotlight and he captained our Under-19s to UEFA Youth League glory, scoring a brace in the final against Shakhtar Donetsk.

He was also part of the Under-18s team which lifted the FA Youth Cup, the youngster netting in the second leg of our final win over Manchester City.

ISAIAH BROWN	
Position: Forward	
Date of birth: 07.01.97	
Place of birth: Peterborough	
2014/15 PREMIER LEAGUE	
Appearances	0+1
Minutes	14
Goals	0
Assists	0

Nathan Ake

Nathan Ake enjoyed a landmark season as he was promoted to the first-team squad by José Mourinho, making appearances in the Champions League, FA Cup and League Cup.

Ake made his Chelsea first-team debut on Boxing Day 2012 in a 1-0 win at Norwich City, coming on as a late substitute, before going on to make a further five appearances that season. He ended the campaign with a place on the substitutes' bench in the Europa League final and won the club's Young Player of the Year award.

After a brief loan spell at Reading in 2015, Ake featured in our penultimate league game of the season away at West Bromwich Albion.

NATHAN AKE	
Position: Defender	
Date of birth: 18.02.95	
Place of birth: Gravenhage, Holland	
2014/15 PREMIER LEAGUE	
Appearances	0+1
Minutes	21
Goals	0
Assists	0

MOURINHO'S MEN

Andreas Christensen

The biggest and best occasion Christensen has been involved in during his career came in the final game of the season against Sunderland as he made his Chelsea league debut.

The Dane came on for John Mikel Obi before John Terry collected the Barclays Premier League trophy – an experience which is bound to have whetted his appetite for future success.

A tall, ball-playing centre-back, Andreas Christensen spent eight years at Brondby before joining Chelsea ahead of many other suitors before the 2012/13 campaign.

He has made a big impact below the first-team with the Under-21s and in the FA Youth Cup but he had to wait until Chelsea's title-winning season to be selected for José Mourinho's side.

He played in the Capital One Cup at Shrewsbury in October 2014 before facing Bradford City in the FA Cup in January 2015.

ANDREAS CHRISTENSEN	
Position: Defender	
Date of birth: 10.04.96	
Place of birth: Allerød, Denmark	
2014/15 PREMIER LEAGUE	
Appearances	0+1
Minutes	14
Goals	0
Assists	0

Wembley winners

Capital One Cup success started the ball rolling

The Premier League trophy wasn't the only piece of silverware Chelsea collected in the 2014/15 season.

Just as in his first spell with the club, José Mourinho kicked off his trophy hunt in England by claiming the League Cup.

While in 2005 the victims were Liverpool at Cardiff's Millennium Stadium, this time it was Tottenham Hotspur that had to be overcome at Wembley, after we'd beaten Bolton Wanderers, Shrewsbury Town, Derby County and the Reds in the earlier rounds.

A glorious day for the club on 1 March resulted in John Terry lifting the Capital One Cup before joyous celebration scenes were played out in front of delirious Chelsea fans on the Wembley turf.

Man-of-the-match Terry's first cup final goal was added to by a Diego Costa strike as Chelsea claimed a 2-0 win.

The deadlock, in what had been a tight encounter, was broken shortly before half-time when the skipper finished off a set-piece. From then on there only looked likely to be one winner and the lead was doubled inside the hour when Diego Costa's drive from the left flicked off Kyle Walker on its way in.

Eden Hazard and Cesc Fàbregas then went close but two goals proved to be enough to win the League Cup for the fifth time in Chelsea history, not least due to a fine defensive display featuring Kurt Zouma in midfield that kept Spurs at bay.

The victory seemed like a landmark moment for Mourinho's new Chelsea team and whetted the appetite for the Premier League success which followed.

CHELSEA (4-3-3):
Cech, Ivanovic, Cahill, Terry, Azpilicueta, Ramires, Zouma, Fàbregas (Oscar 88), Willian (Cuadrado 76), Diego Costa (Drogba 90+3), Hazard.
Unused subs: Courtois, Filipe Luis, Ake, Remy.

TOTTENHAM HOTSPUR: (4-2-3-1):
Lloris, Walker, Dier, Vertonghen, Rose, Bentaleb, Mason (Lamela 71), Chadli (Soldado 80), Eriksen, Townsend (Dembele 62), Kane.
Unused subs: Vorm, Fazio, Davies, Stambouli.

GOALS: Terry 45, Diego Costa 56
ATTENDANCE: 89,297
REFEREE: Anthony Taylor

CAPITAL ONE CUP

JOSE MOURINHO:

"For me it's important to feel like I'm a kid. Before the game I had the same feelings as my first final. It's important to feel the same happiness after the game. I know I have a team to build, which is what we are doing, but it's difficult for me to live without winning things even if we are doing the work to be stable for many years. It's important for me, the boys; and for the club it's another cup.

"I enjoyed Didier Drogba, Petr Cech, John Terry – guys with cups and cups and cups – enjoying it because I see a little bit of myself in that image. You are never tired of winning things.

"I enjoyed the guys that won with Chelsea for the first time or almost for the first time – Hazard, Willian, Oscar, these people.

"And I enjoyed a lot the kids that I know are going to have lots of this in front of them.

"I enjoyed the [happiness of the] fans, my family, and the families of the players. I enjoyed it as much as the first time."

EDEN HAZARD:

"The fans were unbelievable. Every season they wait for trophies because when you play for Chelsea you have to win trophies. The win was for us and for them.

 "We know how important games are against Tottenham for the fans. We lost the last game against them but we deserved to win this time. It's great to bring the trophy back to Stamford Bridge."

CAPITAL ONE CUP

JOHN TERRY:

"Harry Kane has been in great form this season but I thought defensively we were great keeping them at bay.

"The pitch and the atmosphere were amazing; the stadium is one of the best I've ever played in. On a personal note to get the goal, keep a clean sheet, win and lift the trophy – it doesn't come much better than that.

"It is the start of something and we have to win trophies to be up there with some great sides, but we have won our first one now and in 2005 it inspired us and kicked us on and hopefully this will do the same.

"It was fairly even in the first half but we controlled it a little better in the second half and we are deserved winners.

"Spurs like to press, certainly in that first phase, so we tried to miss that out and get the ball into the front man a bit sooner which eliminated it a little bit, and I am delighted for Diego, he is in great goalscoring form and it is great to see him do it on the big stage as well."

Celebration time

With the Capital One Cup won months earlier, the title was wrapped up in May.
So with the Champagne chilling, the ticker tape prepared and the parade bus
engine being warmed up, all we needed was to see a gleaming Barclays Premier
League trophy being lifted by delirious players and staff of our beloved club.
It was time to let the party begin....

CELEBRATION TIME

CELEBRATION TIME

CELEBRATION TIME

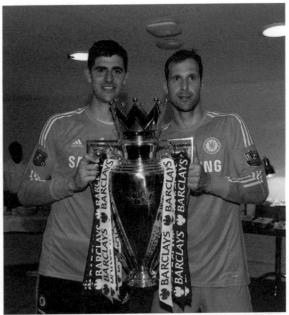

CELEBRATION TIME

CELEBRATION TIME

CELEBRATION TIME

CELEBRATION TIME

AND FINALLY...
SOME INTERESTING STATS FROM A DOMINANT CAMPAIGN

• Chelsea lost only four games all season (in all competitions), a record low for a team in the Premier League era. Interestingly, the four managers to defeat Chelsea in the 2014/15 season all had surnames starting with P: Pardew, Pochettino, Parkinson and Pulis.

• John Terry became the Premier League's all-time highest scoring defender (39).

• Diego Costa became only the fourth Chelsea player to reach 20 goals in a Premier League campaign (after Hasselbaink, Drogba and Lampard).

• Diego Costa reached 10 Premier League goals in just nine games; the only player to reach double figures in fewer is Mick Quinn (six).

• Cesc Fàbregas assisted 18 goals*, only two short of Thierry Henry's single season record of 20 in 2002/03. 18 was a personal record for Fàbregas after his previous best of 17 with Arsenal in 2007/08.

• Eden Hazard missed the 10th penalty he took in the Premier League (his first failure) but scored the rebound [v Crystal Palace].

• Thibaut Courtois kept 12 clean sheets** in his debut Premier League season. Petr Cech kept 24 in his first campaign (04/05).

• Hazard saw 23 opponents booked for fouling him in the Premier League last season.

• On the final day of the season Cech played his 333rd Premier League game for Chelsea; only two goalkeepers have played more for a single club (Jussi Jaaskelainen – 379 for Bolton, Shay Given – 354 for Newcastle).

• Champions Chelsea topped the table for 274 days of the season, a record in the Premier League era. Last season's title winners Man City were top for only 15 days.

• John Terry became only the second outfield player to play every minute for a Premier League title-winning side (along with Gary Pallister in 1992/93).

* Club statistics, which use a different criteria to allocate assists, give him 24 assists.
** Club statistics give him 13 clean sheets, which includes the home game with Arsenal in October when he was substituted due to injury without conceding a goal. Stats in this column from Sky Sports.

Scroll of Honour

THE MANAGER & PLAYERS

JOSE MOURINHO

JOHN TERRY	DIDIER DROGBA	JUAN CUADRADO
EDEN HAZARD	OSCAR	PETR CECH
BRANISLAV IVANOVIC	DIEGO COSTA	RUBEN LOFTUS-CHEEK
NEMANJA MATIC	RAMIRES	MOHAMED SALAH
WILLIAN	LOIC REMY	NATHAN AKE
GARY CAHILL	JOHN OBI MIKEL	ISAIAH BROWN
CESC FABREGAS	FILIPE LUIS	ANDREAS CHRISTENSEN
THIBAUT COURTOIS	KURT ZOUMA	
CESAR AZPILICUETA	ANDRE SCHURRLE	

*Compiled from loyal fans who subscribed to Chelsea FC: Champions 2014-15.
They take their place alongside the manager and every player who contributed to
our successful 2014/15 Barclays Premier League campaign*

SCROLL OF HONOUR

THE FANS

IAN AALPOL
HISHAM ABDEL RAZEK
KEN ABRAMSON
AJIBOLA ABUDU
BART ACCARDO
MARK ADAIR
HENRY ADAMIAK
ANTONI ADAMIAK
CLAIRE AGATHE
ABDULMAJEED AGBOOLA
TEHMINA AHMED
ABDULAZIZ ALARFAJ
ROD ALDRIDGE
ROBERT ALDRIDGE
NICOLAS ALEXANDER
JAMIE ALEXANDER
NAIF ALHAMAM
AMIR J ALIPOUR
JAMES ALLEN
TAYLOR ALLEN
LUCY ALLONBY
JONAS N. ALME
JACK BH ALMOND
LEILA AL-ZUHAIRI
ROSS AMOS
LAURENCE ANASTASI
STEEN HURUP ANDERSEN
MAX ANDERSON
SCOTT GJ ANDERSON
GORDON C ANDERSON
MIKESPIKE ANDERSON
SUE ANDREWS
ARISTOTLE ANTYPAS
STEVE APPLEBY
MUHAMAD ARIF AIZAT
BLAKE ARMSTRONG
FREDDIE.J ARNOLD
KEVIN & ANNA ARTLETT
ATIF ASHARY
TREVOR M ASHLEY
ARJUN ASOK NAIR
CHRISTOPHER ATKINS
NICOLA ATKINS
X ATTAPON
CLIFF AUGER
LUIS & ZACK AULD
DAVID AUSTIN
REECE BACHELOR
KEITH BADGERY
GEORGE BAGLEY
KEVIN BAILEY
CHRISTIAN BAILEY
JACQUELINE BAILEY
PAUL BAILEY
IAN BAILEY

NICHOLAS BAINES
CHRISTOPHER BAKER
JOHN BAKER
FRASER BAKER
DAVID BALDERSTONE
BOBBY BALL
JACK BALSAM
EMILY BALSAM
MARK BAMFORD
DEREK BANISTER
SIMON BANYARD
MARCEL BARAN
JOSH BARBER
KARIS BARFIELD
SHAUN BARKER
MARTIN BARNARD
COLIN & TOM BARNETT
PETER J BARNETT
DAVID BARR
DAVID BARRETT
JOSH & MATTY BARRETT
ARCHIE BARRITT
MICK BARRY
MELVIN BARTOLOME
CHARLOTTE BARTON
NIK BARTRUM
DAVID BARUCH
MATTHEW BATCHELOR
CHESTER BATES
MARK BAXTER
AARON BAXTER
DAVE BEADELL
RYAN J BEALE
PATRICIA BEALES
HARRY BEAR
SAMUEL BEASEY
PAULINE BEER
YANIS BEKS
STEPHEN BELCHER
JOHN BELCHER
ROBERT J BELL
RILWAN BELO-OSAGIE
CHRIS BENGER
TIM BENGOUGH
PER-OLOF BENGTSSON
PAUL J BENNETT
STEVE BERG
MICHAEL BERRY
ANDREW BESSANT
CANDACE & BETTE
MARTYN BETTS
CODY BEVAN
COLIN BIDDULPH
DOUGLAS BIDGOOD
SANDRA BIDWELL

MATTHEW BIGGS
DANIEL BIGGS
KATHARINE BILBROUGH
RAY BILLINGHURST
LAU BILLY BLUES
ALLEN BINGHAM
JEFF BISHOP
MICHAEL BITONIO
LUKE BLACKWELL
KERRY BLAIR
SHANNON BLANCHARD
ANDY BLANCHARD
JOHNNY BLASKETT
ALFIE BLASKETT
LEWIS BLOCK
PETER BLOCK
STEVE BLUEBOY DAY
PETER BLUMIRE
PAUL BLYTH
ANDY BOARD
TONY BOEY
GARY BONNER
NICOLA BONNEYWELL
DANIEL BONNEYWELL
DARREN BONNEYWELL
PAUL BOORMAN
SHAYA BORKENT
DALTON BOTTOMLEY
DAVID BOUCHER
CAROLE & JON BOWERS
PANNY BOXER
TED BOYHAN
DAVID BOYHAN
KAYVON BOYHAN
MIKE BOYLE
KEITH BOYSON
KEVIN BOZMAN
PAUL BRACKLEY
LINDA BRADLEY
LEO JAMES BRADLEY
JACK BRANDON
JON BRAY
PHILIP BREWER
SALLY BRIDLE
KEITH BRISTOW
WILLIAM BROGAN
CRAIG R BROMWICH
PETE BROOD
OSCAR BROOKER
SHAREN BROOKS
MARC BROOKS
COLIN BROOKS
HOLLY BROOKS
MARIANNE BROWN
TRACY BROWN

PAMELA BROWN
JO BROWN
TOBY BROWNING
NEIL N LIAM BRUNNER
KEITH BRUNT
NICK BRUNTON
ADAM BRYANT
THOM BUCKLAND
KEVIN BUCKLAND
SARAH BUCKLEY
LESTER BUCKLEY
ALAN BUDD
JAMES BUDD
GARY BUDDEN
BLUTO BULB
PETE BULL
PETER BURGESS
CALLUM J BURKEY
MARK BURNS
STEVEN BURROWS
JACK BURROWS
IAN BURROWS
KEITH BURROWS
NICK BURROWS
MARGARET BURT
DEBBIE BURTON
ANDREW BUSH
ALAN BUTTOLPH
JAZZ ATESH BUYUKKARACA
AKIN BUYUKKARACA
DANNY CAIGER
BILL CAIN
ANTHONY CALLEJA
MARTIN CALVER
ASHTON CAMERON
FERGUS CAMERON WATT
SCOTT CAMPBELL
MATT CANDERTON
SONIA M CANLAS
REECE CANNON
LLION CARBIS
PHILIP CAREY
MITCHELL CARR
JAMES CARROLL
JILL CARTER
MICHAEL CASSIDY
DAVID CATTINI
JOHN CAVANAGH
GUILLAUME CAZENAVE
SEBASTIEN CHAHBAZI
NORMAN CHAMBERS
ANDREW CHAMBERS
ROBERT CHAMBERS
GRAHAM CHAMBERS
JANET CHAMBERS

THE FANS

JOSH CHAMBERS	GEORGE COX	JIM DELARGY	DANIEL EASTWOOD
LUCAS CHANCELLOR	JOHN COX	PETER DEMETRIOU	RICHARD ECCLESTON
HONG CHANGXI	TOMMY COX	CARL DENT	MIKE EDWARDS
ANDREW CHAPLIN	RON COX	MICHAEL DENTON	CARTER EE
ADAM CHAPMAN	DEREK COX	JOHN DERRIG	SOPHIE EELES
DAVE & TREES CHAPMAN	PHILIP COX	MARK DE-STE-CROIX	MOUSTAFA EL MEHREK
THOMAS CHAPMAN	SCOTT COX	MIKE DETSINY	DIANE ELDER
DANIEL CHARMAN	CONOR CRANLEY	LOUIS W DEWAR	UCHE ANAGHA ELEANYA
MUNYA CHARUMA	RENSTON CRASTA	GEOFF DEXTER	STEWART J ELLIOTT
ELIAS CHEBL	JAMES CRAUFURD	MIEKI D'HAEYERE	STEVE ELPHINSTONE
SIYI CHEN	STEPHEN CRAWFORD	RENE D'HULST	NICHOLAS EMMS
PENNEY CHESTERTON	KYLE CRAWFORD	DANIEL DIACK	JOSEPH ENGLAND
ROYCE CHEUNG	AMANDA CREED	SIMON DIBERNARDO	MAX ENGLISH
MIHAIL CHILARU	JANE CREESE	IAN DICKINSON	JENNY ETHERIDGE
SHIH-YUAN CHIOU	PETER CRISPIN	JAKE DICKSON	CHARLES EUBANKS
SCOTT CHISHOLM	KORBEN CROCKER	BLANE DICKSON	BRYAN EVANS
JOHN L CHISLETT	OLLIE CROFT	JI LAI DING	MATTHEW EVANS
MICHAEL CHRISSI	JOHN CROSTHWAITE	KRAIG DIXON	STEVE EVERITT
GIGS CHRISTODOULO	TONY CULWICK	REX DOBINSON	JOHN EYLES
NICK CHURCHMAN	KIERAN CUMMISKEY	MORGAN DOCHERTY	PHIL FAHEY
LAI CHWING CHURN	SAMUEL CURRIE	KEVIN DODD	PARTRIDGE FAMILY
PAUL CLACK	ISABELLA CURRIE	PATRICK DOEKBRIJDER	ISSAM FARES
PAUL CLARK	CHELSEA CURRIE	HANNAH DOIDGE	STEVE FARROW
JAMIE CLARK	DAISY CURRIE	TYLER DOLAN	FADY AND FATEN
DAVID CLARKE	JOHN CURTIS	ROMAN DOMANSKI	NEIL JAMES FEATHERSTONE
ANTHONY CLARKE	OLIVER B CUTTS	LIAM DOMSALLA	FRANK FELIX
LUCY CLARKE	FONS DAEMS	LEIGH DONALDSON	DAVID FELLOWES
SAM CLARKE	RAYMOND DALCHOW	JACK A F DORMER	MATTHEW FENTON
TONY CLAXTON	LEANNE DANIEL	SUKHJIT DOSANJH	JAMES FERDINAND
WILL CLEIN	PAUL DARMODY	MAUREEN M DOUGLAS	EDDIE FERGUSON
KEVIN CLUSKER	FRANKIE DAVENPORT	COLIN DOURISH	CAMILO FERNANDES
CHELSEA DEBS COADY	CHARLIE DAVEY	ALISTAIR DOURISH	JOSHUA FERRIS
CAROLINE COATES	EDWARD DAVID	NIALL DOURISH	JONNY L FEW
DANNY COLDWELL	DAVID MILLWARD	MALCOLM DOWLMAN	ALEC FIELD
JAMES A COLES	MIKE DAVIES	JUSTIN DOWSE	DEAN FIFIELD
JACKIE COLES	ELLIE DAVIES	PETER A DOYLE	CHUCK FINCH
AIDAN COLLINS	SCOTT DAVIES	CHELSEY DOYLE	PAULINE FINCH
CALUM COLLINS	GARVIN DAVIES	TIM DRAKE	DECLAN FINLAYSON
JON COLVILLE	LEE DAVIES	JOHN DREWITT	FINLAY FISHER
SCOTT CONNELL	SIMON DAVIES	CHARLIE DRIVER	FRANCIS FITCHETT
GEORGE CONNOLLY	CHRISTOPHER DAVIES	ERIC S DUFF	OLIVER FITZGERALD
LORRAINE CONNOR	MIKEY DAVIS	MICHAEL DUKE	OVE FJELLHOY
MICHAEL CONWAY	SUKI DAVIS	ANTHONY DUNNE	LES FLANAGAN
TONY COOKE	MARK DAVY	PAUL DURIE	CONOR FLANNERY
JACK A COOPER	HARRY DAWES	DUNCAN DURMAN	KAVAN FLAVIUS
KATE L COOPER	DAVID ALAN DAY	ANTHONY DWELLY	FLECKY
LEWIS COOPER	HARRY DAY	KEITH DYE	NATHAN FLEETWOOD
DEANO COOPER	JACK DAY	ROBERT DYE	PETER FLYNN
GEORGE J COOPER	VINCE DE FREITAS	RIDZAL DZULKIFLI	JAMES JOHN FLYNN
ALISON COOPER	MARVIN DE FREITAS	PAUL EADY	RAYMOND FONG
JOSH COOPER-ROBER	BJORN DE PAEPE	TERRY EAMES	YIU CHUNG FONG
PATRICK G CORDERY	JOHN DEADY	SARAH EAMES	JOHN FORD
PAUL CORNWALL	SUSAN DEASY	EILEEN EARWAKER	CHARMAINE FORD
PAUL COVE	JAMES DEBATE	JULIAN EASTERBROOK	TREVOR FORD
COLIN COWLEY	YASEEN DEEN	SAM EASTON	ADAM FOREY

SCROLL OF HONOUR

LAWRENCE FORMOSA
JOHN R FORSTER
THOMAS FORSYTH
GEMMA FOWLE
MICHAEL FOWLE
GRAHAM FOWLER
LUKE FOX
MARTIN FOX
ANDREW FRAIN
DAVID FRANCIS
JOHN FRANCIS
JOHN W FRANCIS
SIMON FRANGIOSA
JAMES FRANKLIN
HO KWOK FAI FRANKY
SALLY FRASER
CAMERON FREE
NEIL FREELAND
JOSHUA FREEMAN
CHRIS FREEMAN
CHRISTIAN FRICKEL
JACKSON FRIEDA
THERESE FRIIS
ANTHONY FROST
JACK FUKE
TAKAYUKI FUKUDA
NAO FUKUI
DAVID FULLERTON
JESSICA FUNG
JACK FURBANK
JOHN GAGE
STEVE GAINEY
TOM GALBRAITH
RIC GALE
THOMAS GAMPER
DHVANIL GANDHI
TAO GAO
MEL GARFIELD
MICK GAUCI
OWEN GAUNTLETT
ARUN GAYATRI
MICK GAYLOR
GEORGE GAZE
RYAN GEANEY
JOSEPH P GEDLING
HELEN GELDARD
BEN GERAGHTY
JONATHAN GERKEN
NATHAN GIBBS
BEN GIBLING
TONY GIBSON
WENDY GIBSON
REBECCA GIDDY
ADAM GIDMAN
CAMERON GIESBERS

CAMERON GILBEY
TONY GILES
MICHAEL GILLESPIE
PAUL GILLINGHAM
LUKE GILMOUR
BENJAMIN GILMOUR
CHARLOTTE GIST
NIGEL GLAZIER
OSCAR GLENN
MARK ELVIS GODDARD
MAXIMUS JACK GODLEY
KEVIN GOLDING
BRIAN GOLDSBURY
KATIE GOLDSMITH
RON GOODALL
DAVID A GOODERE
JANET GOODMAN
MATTHEW GOODSON
PATRICK GORDON-BROWN
DAVE GOTT
COLIN GOUGH
JAMES GOULD
LISA-MARIE GOULD
KEVIN GOWER
AMY GOWER
TOM GRACE
MARTIN GRADY
RICHARD GRAHAM
NICK GREEN
JOSH GREEN
PAUL A GREEN
ROBERT M GREEN
MARK GREENAWAY
PAUL GREENAWAY
KYLE GREENE
LORCAN GREENE
NIGEL GREGORY
JOHN GRICE
PAUL GRIFFIN
MILVERTON GRIFFITHS
GEORGE GRIFFITHS
PAUL W GRINDROD
MICK GRIST
DELLA GRIST
GARRY B GROVE
JAMES GUBBINS
UDAY K GUJADHUR
GWYNETH A GUNDRY
RUSHEEL GUPTA
KEVIN GUTCH
JAMES GUTTRIDGE
LEE GUTTRIDGE
GARETH G-WILKIN
PATRICK GYSIN
DANIEL GYTE

NADER M. H. AL-SHAIKH
TRYPHONAS HADJIIOANNOU
CHARLIE HAGGART
CHARLOTTE HAGGIS-BELL
IZAAK N HAINES
STEPHEN M HAINES
MYLAN HAJITHOMAS
CHARLIE HALL
MYLES HALL
SCOTT HALLETT
JOE HAMBLETON
JAKE HAMBLETON
VALERIE HAMILTON
STEPHEN HAMMERSLEY
HARRY HAMPTON
JOHN HANBY
ADAM HANCOX
RAY HANDYSIDE
MICHAEL HANNA BA
PETER J HANSCOMB
NINA E HANSEN
EILEEN HARDING
MARK HARDY
JEZ HARE
VIJAY HARILELA
JAMIE HARPER
THOMAS DAVID HARRIES
MATTHEW HARRINGTON
ADRIAN HARRIS
NEIL HARRIS
NICK HARRISON
NICK HARRISON
SALLY HARRISON
TASHA HARRISON
MARTIN HART
ANDY HART
AMANDA HART
RICHARD HART
ZACH HARTILL
SYLVIA HASLETT
KERI HAWKINS
JOSH HAWKINS
KEVIN HAWKSWORTH
WILLIAM HAYDIS
JOHN HAYES
SEAN HEAD
KEVIN HEATLY
FRANCES HEDINGER
LUKE HELPS
CHARLOTTE HEMINGWAY
HARRI HEMMI
GLENN HENDERSON
GARETH HENRY
JAMES HENSON
WARRICK HERRING

MAURICE HERRING
LAUREN HERRINGTON
RICHARD HEWITT
DEREK HIBBERT
NEIL HICKEY
PAUL HICKMAN
MICHAEL HIGGINS
COLIN HILBOURNE
MARTIN HILDITCH
KEVIN HILL
DANNY HILL
ALLAN HILLY HILL
MAX HILL
ROY HINCHLIFFE
PAUL HINSLEY
DAVID HIPKISS
DANIEL HITERER
DAVID HOCKLEY
MICHAEL HOLLAND
BEN HOLLAND
MICHAEL HOLLAND
DAVID HOLLOWAY
CAMERON HOLM
GEMMA HOLMES
BLAKE HONOUR
ERIC HOOK
JOHN T F HOOLEY
NICK HOPE
JULIE HOPES
MARTIN HORNE
THOMAS HOSKINS
SIMON HOUIS-HAMEAD
NICHOLAS HOWARD
MICHAEL HOWARD
RAYMOND HOWDEN
JACK ARTHUR HOWE
CHARLIE HOWES
ZHENFEI HU
BILL HUBERT
RICHARD HUDSON
IZAAK B HULL
ALAN HUMPHRIES
STEVEN HUMPHRIES
RICHARD HUTCHERSON
SCOTT HUTCHISON
DAVID HUTCHISON
DAVE HUTLEY
FREDDIE HUXTABLE
HAZEL HYAMS
REIKO ICHIKAWA
PETER IDDENDEN
JITHE IDHORODGE
OLIVIA INCE
NIGEL INGRAM
IOAN INGS

THE FANS

JOE IP	ARTHUR KARAMOUZIS	MICHAEL KNIGHT	JAMES LEWIS
GABRIEL IQBAL-SMART	TOHMAS KARLSSON	RAY KNIGHT	CHRISTOPHER LEWIS
SHIBU ISAAC	KLORANDERS KARLSTAD	PETER KNIGHT	NICOLAS LEWIS
KEICHI IWASHITA	RAMONA KARRENBAUER	FRANKIE KNIGHTS	RAYMOND LEWIS
KIMANI JACK	AKSHAT KASAVARAJU	KAYLEIGH KNIPE	KIERAN LEYSHON
SARAH JACKSON	KEN KAUDER	MATTHEW KNOX	SHANGEN LI
TIM JACKSON	LEE KAUDER	KEEGAN KOH	TERRY LI
LACEY JACKSON	STEVEN KAYALICOS	TERUHITO KOMATSU	TIM LIDDIARD
JOHN JACKSON	LIAM KEARNS	DAVID KORN	JOSH LILLE
ARCHIE-EDDIE JACKSON	NEIL KEEBLE	JACQUES KOSMIN	TONY LINDSAY
LEE JANES	RACHEL KEEN	DAVID KOSTIS	OLI LINE
ANDY JANKIEWICZ	JOE KEENAN	JOSEPH KOTVICS	DIANE LISTER
SHIRLEY JARDINE	GRAHAM KELLY	NIPHOT KRAILASOLARN	XIN LIU
HEATHER JARDINE	MIKE KELLY	KOJI KUMAMARU	FRANCIS LOBO
RYAN JEBB	TOM (OSSIE) KELLY	SAPAT KUNAL	KULWINDER LOCHAB
JACK JEE	EAMONN KELLY	MIKHAIL KUPRIYANOV	RAGHU LOGAN
KIAN JOSHUA JEFFRIES	CONOR KELLY	CHATCHAI KWANTHITINAN	DAMIEN LOGAN
JON JENKINS	PETER KEMP	MOUAWIA LABABIDI	MICHAEL LOGUE
YONG HA JEONG	JOSHUA KEMPTON	MARKO LÄHDEAHO	STEVEN LONDON
POWELL JESSAVALA	JAMIE KEMPTON	ANDY LAI	RORY LONERGAN
NIGEL JESSOP	JACK KEMPTON	TOM LAM	KEITH LONG
NUNO JESUS	JAMES KENNEDY	KAI FUNG LAM	EMMANUEL LONGE
AIDAN J JOHN	ADAM KENNEDY	PETER LAMPRELL	LUCA LONGHI
HAYLEY A JOHNSON	DARREN MARK KENNEDY	MARK LAND	ALEX LOPEZ-WILSON
JOHN S JOHNSON	MARK KENT	RICHARD LANE	CALLUM LOUGHRAN
CHARLIE JOHNSON	GRAHAM KEOGHOE	STEPHEN LANE	LEO LOUKOILA
TOM JOHNSON	DAVID KERMAANI	IAN LANGRIDGE	CHRISTOPHER LOWTHER
JACK JOHNSON	LAURA-JANE KERSHAW	MARIE LANNOY	JULIAN LOWTHER
PETER JOHNSON	ANDY KETTLER	ROALD ATLE LARSEN	MATTHEW LUCKIN
PAUL JOHNSON	ZAIN KHALID	CHERRIE LAU	OLIVER LUI
LUCAS JOHNSTON	ZAYAAN KHALID	JONATHAN LAU CHUN HIN	RICO LUIS
TITUS JOHNSTON	MIKHAIL KHARADZHIEV	JONAS LAUREYS	YIN LUNG SZE
COLIN B JOLLIFF	DAVID KILFORD	MATTHEW LAVELLE	MAX LUNN
WILKINS JONALFIEMAX	DUNCAN KILFORD	JENNIFER LAVENDER	TERRY LYALL
MAISIE JONES	DAEKEON KIM	MARCUS C LAWRENCE	PAUL LYNCH
CHARLOTTE JONES	PETER KIMAN	BRANIMIR LAZIC	ROSS LYON
ALEX JONES	JOHN KINCHIN	ANTHONY LEDIEU	DEBBIE LYONS
RYAN JONES	GEEZA KING	ANDREW LEDNIOWSKI	JIM MAAG
WILLIAM J JONES	KINGGY KING	ANDREW LEE	KEITH MABBUTT
KERRY JONES	GARY KING	GYU PYOUNG LEE	STEPHEN MABEY
DAVID ANDREW JONES	LIAM KING	COOPER JACK LEE	KEN MACALPINE
ABIGAIL JONES	ANNE-MARIE KING	FEELING LEE	BENJAMIN MACDONALD
KOTCHAKORN JOOHONG	PAUL J KINGE	JANINE LEES	OSCAR MACGREEVY
THOMAS JORDAN	STEVEN G KINGE	ERROL LEIBA	ADRIAN JASON MACHALEPIS
ERIK JORENS	MICHAEL KIRK	MAREK J LENARTOWICZ	HEATHER E MACINTYRE
SAM JOSEPH	FIONA KIRKUP	JAMES P LENTHALL	MICK MACKAY
KEVIN JOYCE	ANDREW KIRKUP	SAMUEL LEONARD	CRAWFORD MACKAY
GARYCHAN JOYCELIU	MICHAEL KIRKUP	GARY LEONARD	CAMPBELL MACKAY
EDDIE JOYNER	DAVE KITCHER	MARTIN LEONARD	CHRISTIAN MACKAY
HYUNJIN JU	YUTAKA KITO	LUDOVIC LEROY	BEN MACKENZIE
ANDREW JUPP	NINA KJÖREN	CHANTAL LESCURE	IAN MACLEOD
EDMOND K L LAU	JAMES KLONOWSKI	HARRY LESTER	MATTHEW MACPHEE
KRISTOFFER K KAAE	MERYK KLUS-ROBERTS	JONATHAN LEVENE	CHELSEA MAENHOUT
FARRAH KAID	ALEX KNIGHT	PETER LEWIS	ERIC MAENHOUT
KRISHNA KANDEL	JAN KNIGHT	JOSEPH LEWIS	JULIAN MAHER

SCROLL OF HONOUR

HAYDN MAHONEY
RICK MAJKOWSKI
JOHN.W. MAJOR
SPENCER MALONEY
JOSEPH MALONEY
DOMINIC MALONEY
TONY MALTBY
PAUL MANGAN
WILLIAM MANN
LAURIE MANN
SUE MANN
LAUREN MANN
CHARLIE MANN
SIRA MANOROM
MATTHEW MANTLE
ALEX MANTLE
ROLAND MANZETTI
THEODORE MANZI
MICHAEL MANZI
BENJAMIN MANZI
PAUL MARKIDES
MICHAEL MARLOW
DAVE MARLOW
DANIEL MARR
CHRIS MARSH
BERTIE MARTIN
DAVID MARTIN
PAUL MARTIN
DAVID E J MARTIN
KELVIN MASKELL
ROB MASON
STEPHEN PAUL MASSEY
ALAN MATHIAS
JAN ERIK MATHIESEN
GARY MATTHEWS
NICHOLAS MAVROUDIS
DAVE MAYCOCK
MILAN MAYES
DEAN MAYES
ANGELA MAYES
LUKE MAZZAMUTO
BILL MCALISTER
ROBBIE MCCARTHY
BILL MCCORMACK
PATRICK MCCOURT
JOSEPH MCCRORY
JOSEPH MCDERMOTT
PEGGY MCDONALD
ROB MCGEE
TIMOTHY J MCGEEVER
ALAN MCGUINNESS
S.T. MCIVER
ANDY MCKAY
ALAN DAVID MCKAY
DREW F R MCLAGAN

VICTORIA MCLELLAN
NATASHA MCLEOD
SAM MCLEOD
COLIN MCVICKER
ADAM MEAGHER
TONY MEIJER
GERRY MERCHANT
LEO MERRON
ANDREAS MICHAEL
CHUNG TIK MAN MICHAEL
OLLY MIDDLETON
THOMSON MIKE
WILLIAM MILES
JAMIE MILES
CALLUM MILLER
OLLIE MILLIGAN
ROB MILLWARD
SAMUEL MILNE
GARY MIST
CHARLIE MIST
GRAEME MITCHELL
NICK MITCHELL
ALAN MITCHELL
GEORGE MITCHELL
ADRIAN MITCHELL
IAN MITCHELL
THOMAS MITCHELL
OLIVER MITCHELL
NATHAN MIXON
IAN MOFFAT
SHAHRIZAL MOHD
SIU LUN MOK
JOSH MONACO
OSCAR MONGEY
MICHAEL MONK
TOEY MONTACHAI M
LUKE MOORE
PETER MORELL
ROGER MORETON
CHARLIE MORRIS
PAUL MORRIS
JAMES MORRISONLAMB
JAMES MORRISONLAMB
JORDAN MORTIMER
ALAN MOSES
DEREK MOSS
STEPHEN MOYLE
TIMVENJI MUHAMBA
TERENCE
JOHN MULHOLLAND
JOHN MULLIGAN
LINDA MULLIN
JAVIER MULVOY-TEN
MALCOLM MUNT
DAVID MURE

RYAN DAVID MURPHY
MICHAEL MURPHY
PETER MURPHY
ALAN MURRAY
ADRIAN MURZE
DAVID MUTTITT
T NAPAS
TOBY NAPLETON
CATHERINE NASH
JOHN NAUGHTON
BELMONT NDEBELE
KEN NEALE
DARIUS NEEDHAM
JOSH NEIMAN
STEPHEN NELKEN
SUSIE NESS
MALCOLM NEWING
GRAHAM D NEWNHAM
ZURIEL NG
MATTHEW NG
OCEAN NG
SUE NICHOLLS
JACKIE NICHOLLS
MICHAEL NICOLA
ALASTAIR NICOLSON
ELLIOTT M NIMMO
ASHLEY J. NOAD
KERRY MARIE NOBLE
LEN LEDGEY NODAROS
PAIGE NORGATE
KEVIN NORLEY
JOSH NORTON
PETER NOYCE
THOMAS N-SMITH
ANTONIO NUNZIANTE
BHARADITYA NURADIMAS
LITA NURMISARI
LIAM O BRIEN
CIAN O'BYRNE
CHRIS O'CONNOR
ROBERT P O'BOYLE
DANNY O'BRIEN
GILLIAN O'CALLAGHAN
DANNY O'CONNOR
JAMIE ODELL
AIDAN O'DONNELL
JIMMIE O'DONNELL
HILARY OGBONNA
LEWIS K OGIER
ABOLAJI OGUNMOLA
DAVE O'HAGAN
MICHELE OHALY
MUGREN OHALY
SIXTEN ÖHMAN
KAZUMASA OHSUGA

MARK OLDEN
STEPHEN OLDHAM
JOHN OLSEN
KEVIN OMAHONEY
DAVID ONEILL
LUKE JOHN O'NEILL
VIOLET & OSCAR PENDER
PAUL W OSGOOD
GEORGE OSMOND
OKEY OTURU
DAVE OWEN
SUSIE P
LEIGH PADLEY
BRIAN PAGAN
JONATHAN PAGE
JASON PAGE
KEVIN PAINE
JONATHAN PALAYA
STEPHEN PALMER
ALAN PAMMENT
GEORGE PANAYIOTOU
REBECCA PANTANEY
DON PANTER
JACK PAPASAVVA
ROGER PAPWORTH
PETER PARKER
GARY PARKIN
LIAM T PARMENTER
TED J J PARMENTER
JOHN D PARMENTER
JOHN D T PARMENTER
MAX E PARMENTER
DANIEL PARR
COLIN PARSONS
MICHAEL J PARSONS
BARRY PARSONS
HOWARD PASK
UJAL PATEL
TABASSUM PATEL
SAFURA PATEL
VIBSPREMMINI PATEL
HARRY PATEY
ANNIE PATEY
NEIL PATIENCE
BRAHM PATTNI
MICHALOWSKI PAUL
MICHAEL PAUL
BLAIR PAUL
CHRISTOPHER PAUL
DAVID PAYN
BEN PAYNE
KENNETH L PAYNTER
LINDA PAYNTER
JAMES PEACOCK
ADAM PEAKE

THE FANS

JORDAN C PEARCE	JAY PURCELL	MAX ROSSITER	WEI SHI
MARTIN PEARCE	JACK PURSEY	ALEX ROWE	KOUHEI SHIOMI
DAVID PEARSON	GRAHAM QUICK	COLIN F ROWE	JACK SHIPTON
CHRIS PEARSON	JAMIE RADCLIFFE	GERARD RUANE	ALISTAIR SHORT
THOMAS PEASE	VELI-MATTI RAES	MARTIN RUCK	GRAHAM D SHORT
LORENZO PEDRETT	NANAE RAI	DARREN RUFF	JARED SHORT
LILIANA PEDRETT	CHUNG MAN YAN RAINBOW	DARIUS RUKAS	LIONEL SHUFENG
CHRISTOPHER PENDER	DINESH RAMSINGH	PAUL RUMBLES	HARRY SIDERAS
STEVE PENDLETON	MARK RANSOM	GRAHAM RUSSELL	ZHI XIANG SIMON YEE
PAMELA PENDLETON	STEVEN RAPLEY	LESLEY RUSSELL	KENNETH SIMONS
JAMES PENFOLD	JOSHUA RASMUSSEN	KEVIN RYAN	LUCIE SIMPER
COLIN PEREIRA	CLARE RAY	CHARLIE RYAN	OLIVER SIMPSON
JOHN PERRY	GEORGIE RAYNER	RYLANDS	GRAEME SINDLE
TYLER-REECE PERSAD	JACK READ	HARRI SAARINEN	JOANNA SINDLE
IAN PETERS	DARYL READ	YOAV SAGI	RICK SINGH
JOSH PETERS	DAVE READ	CHRISTIAN SAKSHAUG	GARY SIRETT
TARA PETERS	JAMES REAR	SHYAM SAMRAJ	BJÖRN ARVE SJÖHOLT
INGRAM PETERS JR	ALI REDHA	PAUL SANDERS	JASPER SKINNER
MARY PHELPS	RICHARD REECE	PAUL SANDFORD	LEWIS SLATER
PAUL PHILLIPS	JAMES REES	MARK SANDOM	KEITH SLAVIN
MATTHEW RG PHILLIPS	JAY REES	BORIS VEGA SARET PULIDO	ROBERT SLYE
GARY PHILLIPS	GRAEME REEVES	VICKY SAUNDERS	JOHN SMART
KERRY PHILPOT	GILL REEVES	JOEL SAUNDERS	SUE SMITH
KERRY PHIMISTER	LEANNE REID	HARRY SAUNDERS	IAN & JASON SMITH
MELVIN PHUANG	ALISON REID	JOHN SAWYER	JASON SMITH
KYAN PICKERING	HARRY REID	MARTYN SCHLAEFLI	ED SMITH
TERRY PIERCE	JOHN REIDY	ELIOTT SCHMITE	DEAN SMITH
GEOFFREY PIGOTT	JAMES REILLY	JOSA SCHNELL	IAN SMITH
PHOEBE PIKE	JULIA REVELL	GRAHAM SCHOLES	ALFIE SMITH
ELOISE PIKE	DANIEL REY	THOMAS SCHUSTER	STEVEN SMITH
MILES PIKE	KAYDEN RICE	STEVE SCOTT	JAMES SMITH
GEORGIA PIKE	EDDIE RICHARDS	KEITH SCOTT	YUJI SODA
WARREN PILOSSOF	ED RICHARDS	PHIL SCOTT	ANDY SOESTER
CLIVE PLANT	COLIN RICHARDSON	CAMERON SCOTT	PAUL SOUTHEY
KEVIN J PLAYLE	JAMES RICHARDSON	WILLIAM SCROPE	NICK SOUTHGATE
LYNNETTE PLUMB	PAUL RIDE	JOSEPH SCUTERI	PAUL SOUTHWICK
DAVID POCOCK	DAVID RIGBY	SYBS SEABRIGHT	PAUL SPENCELEY
DOROTHY POPPLEWELL	DAVID RIGBY	DAVE SEABROOK	PHILIP SPENCER
TIM PORTELLI	STEVEN RING	TOM SEABROOK	ANTHONY SPENCER
ADDISON POST	PAULA RIOME	REBECCA SEALS	IAN SPINKS
LISA POTTER	DAVID ROBERTS	CHRIS SEARLE	PRASHANTH SREE KUMAR
DEREK J POULTON	KEITH ROBINSON	STEPHEN SEDGWICK	MAISIE STAFFORD
LUCAS POWELL	ADAM ROBINSON	PAUL A SEERY	DANIEL STALL
SCOTT POWELL	BEN ROBINSON	DAVID SELLEY	SHAUN STAMPS
WILLIAM POWELL	GARY ROSS ROBSON	MICHAEL SENTER	REBECCA STANCLIFFE
COLIN POWELL	ROWAN ROBSON	SAM SEYMOUR	FRANCES STANLEY
RICHARD POWER	DAVID ROBSON	IAN SEYMOUR	GEORGIA STANLEY
JOHN PREEDY	JOHN RODENHOUSE	PAUL MICHAEL SHALLCROSS	JOHN STARES
JAMES M PRESTON	ALAN H RODERICK	JUSTINE SHAPIRO	BRIAN D STARR
ALAN PRETLOVE	MIKE ROESER	LEE SHARP	ALAN WILLIAM STEEL
MICHAEL PRICE	YEHUDAH ROITENBARG	MACIEK SHASHA	TOM STENSON
BARRY PRICE	LUCA ROMERO	MATTHEW SHAW	GARETH STENT
DELL PRICE	JOSEPH ROMERO	BLUE SHEARS	MILES STEPHENS
RUBY ROSE PRIOR	JOHN ROSE	PAUL SHEPHERD	BRADLEY STEUER
RHYS PROSSER	STEVE ROSE	PAUL SHERIDAN	RICHARD STEVENS